PART II
PASS FOR PROMOTION
FOR SERGEANTS AND INSPECTORS

Jane's

Further titles available:

- Part I Promotion Crammer for Sergeants and Inspectors
- The Beat Officer's Companion
- The Traffic Officer's Companion
- The Scottish Beat Officer's Companion

To order or for further details
phone +44 (0) 20 8700 3700 or fax +44 (0) 20 8763 1006

© Jane's Information Group 2006

1st edition 2006

ISBN 978 07106 2779 7

Jane's Information Group
Sentinel House
163 Brighton Road
Coulsdon
Surrey CR5 2YH

Design and typesetting by utimestwo, Northamptonshire
Graphics: Eyes Down
Front cover images: Empics

Printed and bound in Great Britain by Hobbs the Printers

CONTENTS

INTRODUCTION

Congratulations on your success at Part I of your promotion examination. Now for your Part II assessment centre – a totally different experience. However, rest assured that you are about to undertake one of the fairest and most objective methods of assessment. You will take part in interactive exercises specifically designed for and relevant to the rank subject of your assessment centre. Whilst doing this you will be assessed objectively by fully trained assessors and fully trained role actors will help facilitate this process.

No doubt you will have studied for six months or so to prepare for your Part I and, in doing so, perhaps following a strict study timetable based on the four law manuals and the Part I syllabus.

But how do you prepare for seven interactive role-related work sample exercises? It is your interaction with the role actor that will be assessed and how you deal with the issues contained within an exercise.

This book has been designed to help you prepare for those seven interactions, whether you are preparing for the constable to sergeant or sergeant to inspector Part II.

The seven exercises relating to whichever Part II you are preparing have been designed to relate to that rank. There is no purpose in providing you with exercises that do not reflect the rank. Each exercise will comprise of three parts; candidate information, role-actor instructions and assessment checklist. The candidate information for each exercise will contain different forms of information for you to deal with. This may be in the form of a memorandum, charts containing statistics, an e-mail or graphs.

However, before introducing you the exercises and the way they can help your preparation I want to cover the background to the Part II. This will give you an insight into the process and just how fair a system of assessment it is.

The following points will be covered in this introductory chapter:

- Terminology used through the book
- How you will be assessed
- The competencies relating to both ranks
- How the exercises are designed

- What happens at an assessment centre
- The Divisional Profile
- Contamination

Explaining terminology

The Part II assessment centre is not a game. You do not have to come out with buzz-words or management speak. I have heard candidates waste up to a minute of their time because someone has told them to start each exercise with a structured or set statement or use terms such as:

- 'I value your input';
- 'The police are here to serve the public';
- 'My door is always open'; and
- 'Integrity, it is not just a word you know';

The Part II assessment centre is more sophisticated than parroting a string of meaningless phrases. In fact, the feedback provided to candidates following the assessment centre outlines that it is the weaker candidates who use terms similar to those mentioned above.

You will see why this is the case and why buzz-words or phrases do not play a part when I explain the exercise design process later in this chapter.

The underpinning principle of the Part II assessment centre is to:

'assess your potential to perform in the next rank'

This is why it is essential when you are preparing for your Part II that you approach the exercises from the perspective of the rank subject of your Part II assessment centre. If, for example, you are a candidate for the constable to sergeant assessment centre and one of the exercises requires you to address the under performance of a constable and you do not approach the issues from the perspective of a sergeant you will not properly address the under performance and the opportunity to display your potential in that exercise will be wasted.

I have already mentioned some terms used in the process. I now want to give you an explanation of these terms. This will be useful not only to familiarise you with the terms but will assist when you move onto the exercises and debriefs contained in the book.

Exercises: These are the seven interactive role-related work sample scenarios you will undergo at the assessment centre.

They were once referred to as 'stations'. Some people still refer to them as stations but they haven't been referred to by that name since they were printed on parchment – so we'll use the correct name.

Assessment Checklist: This is the document the assessor uses to assess you throughout your five-minute interaction with the role actor. Assessment checklists contain the competency areas that have been identified during the exercise design process as being best suited to that exercise. I will explain this further when I explain the exercise design process.

All the checklists cover the relevant competency areas, each of which contain behavioural statements. You score the behavioural statement when you say that certain statement.

Each checklist will have a minimum of 12 behavioural statements and a maximum of 18 spread across the various competency areas. Each competency area will contain between three to six behavioural statements. The assessment checklist is broken down in this way for two reasons; it is achievable for you the candidate and does not overload the assessor. However, the Respect for Race and Diversity competency area does not contain specific behavioural statements as you are assessed across the entire five minutes in this competency area. I will explain this in more detail when we examine the competency areas.

The checklist also contains something called scalars. Remember, behaviours are what you say; scalars are how you say it. Scalars are assessed on a bi-polar scale of 1- 5, with 1 being positive and 5 being negative. At the start of the five-minute interaction you commence on a 3 scalar and move up or down the scalar depending on how you score the behavioural statements in that competency area.

To better illustrate this process I will use a behavioural statement that states; *Outlines options to address problems of youth disorder.*

For example, candidate A may say to the role actor: 'I'll have a police officer have a look as they're passing the place where the youths congregate.' Candidate A has outlined a weak option to address the youth disorder situation and if the bi-polar scalar for the competency area was 'thorough to superficial', I'm sure you will agree that the candidate could have done more. Consequently a low scalar of 4, possibly 5, for that particular behavioural statement would be awarded.

However, candidate B outlines the following options to the role actor: 'I'll put targeted patrols in the area and at the same time run a campaign in the local schools. If that doesn't work I can organise some covert observations in an effort to arrest the offenders.' Candidate B has been more thorough in suggesting options to address the youth disorder. Consequently a high scalar of 2 certainly, and possibly 1, would be awarded.

But the Part II assessment process is so fair that should candidate A at some point during their five minute interaction with the role actor return to the options and make further suggestions (not by just repeating their original option) to address the youth disorder they would move further up the scalar for that individual behavioural statement.

At the end of the five minute interaction your final grade, A – D, for each competency area (except Respect for Race and Diversity) is a calculated by the number of behaviours scored; what you say, combined with the overall scalar; how you say it.

If a competency area contains three behavioural statements and a candidate scores two of the three behavioural statements, they would be awarded, overall, a 3 scalar for that competency area. The assessor would award a B grade for that competency area. This may surprise you. You will have noted that the candidate has 'missed' one of the behavioural statements and has only achieved a 'middle of the road' scalar of 3. Should a candidate not score any behavioural statements in a competency area, then that candidate will remain on a 3 scalar, as at the start of the five-minute interaction, and will be awarded a D grade for that competency area.

Assessor/Role Actor: To qualify as an assessor a person has to successfully complete a week-long pass/fail assessor's course. The course instructs people how to assess using the Part II assessment and role acting methodology. The five-minute interaction is not a test for a role actor to use as many lines as possible from their set script. A specific line will only be delivered when the candidate has provided the correct prompt.

Note that they are called role actors and not role players as they have a set script that they must follow (each exercise contained in this book contains role actor instructions outlining the role actor background and script). The fact that a role actor follows a set script ensures consistency and fairness to all candidates undertaking the Part II assessment centre.

If the method of role playing was adopted, the person performing the role playing would be at liberty to follow a demeanour and deliver lines of their choice. This would seriously affect the consistency in the delivery of the exercise and consequently advantage or disadvantage some candidates. The fairness of the assessment method would then be diminished and subsequently it's objectivity as an assessment method affected.

At the assessment centre, assessors and role actors alternate daily between the roles and receive a full day's training in their allocated exercise before they meet candidates. They must be competent in both assessing and role acting before they are allowed to meet candidates. If they do not reach a certain level of competence they will not meet candidates and are released from the assessment centre. The gender or ethnicity of a role actor has no bearing on the exercise unless it is specified in the candidate information. The assessor is in charge of the exercise. If you dry up they will intercede with the comment 'Candidate, you still have time remaining in your five minutes'. You are not penalised for drying up. Likewise you do not have to display a structured approach. If you say a behavioural statement during the 5-minute interaction you will score it.

The competencies

From 1996 the Part II exercises were designed around the competencies contained within Home Office Circular 43 of 1996 (HOC 43/96). However, in 1999 it was considered that the competencies contained in this document no longer reflected those required of a modern police service. Consequently, work commenced on the design of a National Competency Framework for the police service. Thus the Integrated Competency Framework was introduced to the service in April 2001.

Subsequently, the Integrated Competency Framework was introduced to the Part II at the 2004 Inspectors' Part II Assessment Centre.

The competencies relating to the Part II are:

- Community and Customer Focus
- Effective Communication
- Maximising Potential
- Planning and Organising
- Problem Solving
- Resilience (constable to sergeant Part II only)

- Personal Responsibility (sergeant to inspector Part II only)
- Strategic Perspective (sergeant to inspector Part II only)
- Respect for Race and Diversity

In respect of these competencies let me firstly dispel a myth that appears to have become established over the years; you do not have to identify the competency areas that you feel relate to an exercise. This is both during the preparation phase and during the interaction phase.

When you commence the exercises contained in this book you will see why this is the case. During the preparation phase you do not have time to do this and it is not necessary.

Similarly, you do not have to point out to a role actor and/or assessor which competency area you feel you are now addressing. For example, you have information that an officer from your team is under performing in a certain aspect of their work. You do not have to say to that officer, 'I'm now going to maximise your potential'. Some candidates are instructed to say this as it shows the assessor that the candidate has identified the correct competency area. Frankly, this gives you no advantage whatsoever. You will have identified the competency area by suggesting measures to address the under performance. That is how you "score" items on an assessment checklist. I will cover this in greater depth later in this chapter when I explain how you are assessed.

Consequently I do not intend to cover the competency areas individually and extensively. You do need to be aware of them but you do not need to know them back to front.

I do, however, want to spend some time reviewing the Respect for Race and Diversity competency area.

The reason for this being that it is assessed in all seven exercises and, theoretically, being awarded a grade D in this area could result in you failing the Part II overall.

Respect for Race and Diversity: As I have mentioned previously, the Respect for Race and Diversity competency area is assessed in every exercise so it is worth spending bit of time examining the area in some depth.

This competency area differs from the others in that it does not contain behavioural statements. You are assessed against two bi-polar scalars, again as with the other competency areas the scalar is 1-5, across the entire five-minute interaction. So, unlike the other competency areas, where it is possible to improve your scalar for an individual behavioural statement, in the Respect for Race and Diversity competency area you can move up and down the scalar depending on what you say and how you say it. Your final grade is then calculated by the assessor on the two scalars you are awarded. Examples of scalar descriptors in this area for example could be;

- Considerate – inconsiderate
- Supportive – unsupportive
- Objective – biased

Unfortunately, when dealing with a member of the public who has not received the treatment expected from a police officer, it is true that a small minority of candidates believe that the police can do no wrong or should not apologise if a mistake has been made by a peer or an officer for whom they have responsibility. In other words they are biased and/or inconsiderate and the assessor will assess them accordingly.

Similarly when dealing with an officer for whom they have management responsibility and who has under performed, some candidates believe that the correct way to deal with the person is to focus on the under performance. They will concentrate on imposing punitive measures as they believe this is the most constructive way to deal with the under performance. However, what they fail to discover is the reason why the officer is under performing and are thus unable to address that reason.

Contrary to popular belief, assessors are not provided with a definitive list of words or phases that constitute a negative performance in Respect for Race and Diversity. If this were the case, the assessor would have to look through an exhaustive list whilst assessing and that would disadvantage the candidate who is still dealing with the exercise and potentially scoring behavioural statements in the other competency areas.

The assessors are trained to identify unacceptable language or behaviour in the Respect for Race and Diversity competency area. The unacceptable language or behaviour is outlined in Schedule 1 of the Police (Conduct) Regulations 2004. This defines unacceptable language or behaviour as "any language or behaviour which falls short of the standards expected of a police officer".

My advice would be to treat people as you would expected to be treated as a member of the public, or by a line manager or supervisor.

Exercise design process

Let me assure you that every one of the seven exercises you will undertake at your Part II assessment centre follows a comprehensive and robust six-month design process. This is undertaken to ensure that the exercises are fair, relevant to the rank and achievable. All the exercises are written by fully qualified Part II assessment centre exercise design writers.

However, let me stress that you do not have to resolve an exercise in the five minutes you have with the role actor. That would be unfair and unrealistic. Quite obviously if, for example, a constable came to you with a problem during your normal tour of duty it is likely that you would take longer than five minutes to deal with, and resolve, the issues.

Now you may wonder what has the design process got to do with you as a candidate. But having knowledge of the key phases will help you appreciate why it is important to get into the role of a sergeant or inspector.

The initial phases of the design process involve a lot of desktop research into possible exercise ideas. A task analysis of sergeant or inspector rank is conducted. In this way, the most common types of issues a sergeant or inspector has to deal with are identified. Consequently this ensures that the issues contained in an exercise are relevant to the rank subject of the assessment centre. It would be unfair to provide candidates with seven exercises that were not designed to assess their potential in the rank to which they aspire.

Once the exercise ideas have been researched, the exercise writers then conduct critical interviews with identified post holders (sergeants or inspectors). They will ask the interviewee for details of incidents they have dealt with that correlate with information obtained from the rank task analysis. Critical interviews may also be conducted with organisations external to the police service in order to obtain an external perspective of an incident which may be useful when writing exercises which require a non-police role actor. The seven assessment centre exercises are based on actual incidents or issues dealt with by a sergeant or inspector and it is for this reason that the assessment centre exercises are realistic.

Initial exercise trial: This is the first stage of the design process that tests the exercises in an assessment centre environment. The process involves 10 volunteers of sergeant or inspector rank actually undergoing the exercises as candidates. All of the interactions are video taped to enable the exercises to be reviewed. The volunteers are asked to provide feedback regarding relevance to rank, fairness to candidates and whether or not five minutes is sufficient to read through the candidate information contained within the exercise. The videos are subsequently reviewed to establish if the role actor script is sufficient to cover the needs of the exercise.

Group discussions: These are structured group discussions involving Part II assessors and officers of the rank subject of the assessment centre. The group read through all material and comment on the relevance to the rank, fairness to candidates, the realism of the exercises and whether they contain any regional or force differences or specific terminology. This is a point worth noting for you as the candidate. Ensure that you do not use any terminology or phrases peculiar to your own force. Remember the Part II assessment centre is not based in your force but in a fictitious one. In this way no one set of candidates will have an unfair advantage or perceived advantage over other candidates. Should you use terminology from your own force it could result in the assessor not understanding you, assessors in the non-police exercises may be external to the police service, and will therefore not be able to assess you accordingly.

Perhaps I can illustrate this better with an example. Your force has Community Beat Managers (CBM) responsible for policing a local area. As an option to address a problem of local youth disorder you say to the role actor: 'I'll tell you what I'll do to help you, I'll send the CBM down to have a look.' Firstly the force in which the Part II is based may not have Community Beat Managers and secondly the assessor may not know what a CBM is so cannot assess you accordingly. My advice is to stay clear of using terminology or jargon.

Pilot: This stage is usually held in the north of the country to allow forces from that area to contribute to the design process. It is the first real test of the exercises and involves up to 20 volunteer candidates of the rank subject of the assessment centre. The volunteers actually deal with the exercises under the assessment centre timings and conditions. As with the initial exercise trial, once again all of the interactions are video taped and the volunteers are asked for feedback on the same issues of relevance to the rank, fairness to the candidates and whether the candidate information could be completed within the time constraints of the assessment centre.

Checklist design: This is an important stage of the design process and one that you should be aware of as it is this assessment checklist that will be used to assess you.

All of the interactions at the pilot stage are video taped and during the checklist design process the exercise design team works in pairs and views all of the videotapes. In doing so they record on a computer spreadsheet everything that a candidate says to the role actor.

These are the behavioural statements I mentioned earlier in the chapter. Once all 20 videotapes have been viewed and the behavioural statements recorded the total could be between 400 to 600. These behavioural statements are then considered as to their criticality in how a candidate deals with the exercise. Consequently phrases along the lines of 'my door is always open' and 'I value your contribution' will be removed. They are not critical as to how a candidate should deal with the issues contained in an exercise. The remaining behavioural statements are then reviewed and merged. To illustrate this, refer back to the example I quoted earlier in the chapter of *Outlines options to address problems of youth disorder.*

During the pilot stage one candidate may suggest using the Community Support Officers (CSOs) to address the problem. Another may suggest addressing the problem using high visibility uniform officers to patrol the area. Any suggestion offered by the volunteers during the pilot stage to address the problem will be collated and merged into the one behavioural statement as mentioned above.

All of the behavioural statements are then classified under the competency area deemed appropriate to that behavioural statement. The resultant checklist will contain approximately 70 to 100 behavioural statements.

Remember, each competency area (except Respect for Race and Diversity) is measured a minimum of three times across all seven exercises and no exercise contains more than five competency areas.

Validation: The validation stage is similar to the pilot stage. The seven exercises are now in the final format as they will appear in the actual assessment centre. Obviously if the exercise content was changed at this stage it would have a detrimental effect on the exercise checklist as any alterations would not have appeared at the pilot stage and would not have had the opportunity to appear on the exercise assessment checklist.

The validation stage is conducted in a similar way to the pilot stage. It is conducted in the south of the country to give forces from that area an opportunity to contribute to what is a national assessment centre. At this stage, up to 20 volunteer candidates of the rank subject of the assessment centre undertake the process. Once again all the interactions are conducted within the time constraints of the assessment centre and all are video taped.

Checklist Refinement: This is the final stage of the development of the exercise assessment checklist.

Once again the exercise design team work in pairs. During this stage they will review all of the videotapes from both the pilot and validation stages. The behavioural statements that form the assessment checklist from the checklist design stage are "scored" on the spreadsheet as candidates say them on the videotapes. The frequency with which they are scored determines whether or not they appear on the final assessment checklist.

A rather basic way of explaining this is to refer to something called the 80 – 20 rule. This rule works as follows: if 80 per cent or more of the volunteer candidate score the behavioural statement, it is deemed too easy. Likewise if 20 per cent or less score the behavioural statement it is deemed too difficult. The remaining behavioural statements should then be fair to all candidates and be able to discriminate between candidates.

The behavioural statements will then undergo statistical analysis by an occupational psychologist who is part of the exercise design team. The occupational psychologist, exercise writer and team leader then review the results. A behavioural statement achieved by 50 per cent of the volunteer candidates is the perfect behavioural statement as it has the power to discriminate between candidates. These results will dictate the final assessment checklist, which will contain no less than 12 and no more than 18 behavioural statements.

All the exercises and checklists are then presented to the independent moderators and the Race and Diversity monitor and signed off as fit for the assessment centre.

By the end of the design process, between 50 to 70 police personnel will have had an input. I'm sure you will agree that it is fair to say this is a robust process, underpinned throughout by fairness to candidates and relevance to the rank subject of the assessment centre.

It is essential that you get into the role of being a sergeant or inspector as they are the people that, in essence, have compiled the assessment checklist against which you will be assessed.

The important issue for you to remember as a candidate is that all seven exercises are based on actual incidents relevant to the rank to which you aspire and that the assessment checklists relate to the way people of that rank deal with the exercises.

Every exercise will have a couple of issues to address and the clues to those issues are contained in the candidate information. You will be assessed as to how you deal with those issues. Remember you do not have to resolve the issues within five minutes. The purpose of Part II assessment centre is to display your *potential* to perform in the next rank. You only have seven five-minute opportunities to do this. Make the most of the time and don't waste it with meaningless phrases. I'm sure once you have undertaken the exercises contained within this book you will have a greater appreciation of this.

The assessment centre

I now want to look at what happens to you at the actual assessment centre and explain some rules that you should be aware of which will prevent you from any unnecessary hassle or stress on the day. It is not as bad as you may have been lead to believe by those that have already attended the process – after all they are still around to recount their day.

I want to reassure you that you will undergo a very fair and objective assessment process at the heart of which are the candidate's best interests.

Arrival

When you arrive at your allocated assessment centre you will be met by a member of the Centrex examinations and assessment administration team who will collect you from an assembly point that will be clearly signposted. You are then taken into a briefing room to be registered along with up to 13 other candidates. Do not forget your warrant card. If you do you will not be allowed to undergo the assessment centre. For those of you undertaking the inspectors' assessment centre ensure that your warrant card has been updated to the rank of sergeant. This may sound obvious, but it has happened to some candidates. It will prevent delay in your registration as a member of the Centrex examinations and assessment administration team will have to verify with your home force that you are eligible, by virtue of your rank, to undertake the assessment centre. This will only cause you unnecessary delay and stress at the registration process.

When registering, if you have any issues that you feel may have an effect on your performance, mention this to the person carrying out the registration process and they will put you in touch with the candidate co-ordinator who will speak to you in private.

Upon registration you will be issued with a label bearing your candidate number and a room number. The label will also have either a blue or red stripe as the assessment centre floor is divided into a red and blue assessment team. Ensure that you take notice of your room number and stripe colour. Once registered, you will remain in the briefing room to be briefed by the candidate co-ordinator.

Briefing
This is a scripted briefing delivered at a specified time. The running of the assessment centre is timed to the minute hence the logistics have to be extremely well structured. The candidate co-ordinator will explain the logistics of the assessment centre and give you a briefing card. Once you have read this, the candidate co-ordinator will escort you to the actual assessment centre corridor.

Assessment centre corridor loading
Once at the assessment centre corridor you will be given an opportunity to leave all of your personal belongings in a cloakroom. The assessment centre rules do not allow for any documentation, mobile telephones, pagers or other personal belongings to be taken onto the assessment centre corridor. Also ensure that you switch off the bleeping sound emitted by some stopwatches or timers. This is a common problem at the assessment centre and you will be in breach of the rules if you do not. The reason for this is that in the past the sound emitted by stopwatches or timers has been mistaken as the sound emitted by the buzzer used to control the assessment centre timings.

Before actually entering the assessment centre corridor the candidate co-ordinator will line you up in a specific order. It is important at this point that you know your room number and stripe colour. You will then enter the corridor and stand outside the room that matches your room number and stripe colour.

Preparation phase
Do not enter your room until the assessment centre buzzer sounds. It may sound obvious but make sure you sit in the chair marked candidate! The chair marked role actor will be in front of the chair marked candidate. You will also see two other chairs marked assessor and

observer. These two chairs will be placed behind you in a corner of the room out of your eye line. This is so you are not distracted by the assessor during your interaction with the role actor.

Your candidate information booklet containing all seven exercises will be in your room. The front cover will show the order in which you will deal with the seven exercises. The booklet is compiled in that order so there is no need to keep flicking through the booklet to find your next exercise and to assist you the pages are numbered. However, ensure when you are reading through your candidate booklet you do not skip a page. This has occurred in the past. To assist you further an exercise running order is on the wall in front of you.

Once in the room, start your preparation phase immediately. You will remain in this room throughout and have a total of 45 minutes' preparation time. After 43 minutes the assessment centre buzzer will sound informing you that in two minutes time the first role actor and assessor will enter your room. You have roughly six minutes of preparation time per exercise, however, some may contain more candidate information than others. The exercise design process ensures that there is sufficient time to read through the exercise candidate information.

Do not start to panic about the time. You will become preoccupied by it and it will affect your preparation. You may find it helpful to use a highlighter pen to assist you in identifying information you may want to confirm, clarify or mention to the role actor, but do not overdo it and stick to highlighting the relevant words. You do not need to virtually rewrite the exercise. The exercise design team have written it for you. Your notes will not be assessed; only you need to be able to read them.

A recent trend with some candidates during the preparatory phase is to verbalise the content of the exercises as they read through them. Do not do this as you will be in breach of the rules and someone will enter your room and ask you to stop, as you may be disturbing candidates around you. This will disturb your preparation. The assessment corridor is quiet and noise does travel to adjacent rooms.

Activity phase

You have five minutes with a role actor per exercise. This is interspersed with two-minute intervals. Use the two minutes to refresh your memory of the exercise you will be dealing with next. The role actor will be the first person to enter the room, followed by the assessor and by an observer who is there to oversee the exercise, not you as a candidate. There is no need to shake the role actor's hand unless you feel you want to. You will not be marked down if you do not shake their hand. Concentrate on the role actor, they are your other source of information. When the assessment centre buzzer sounds at the end of the five minutes the role actor and assessor will leave the room immediately even if you or the role actor are in mid-sentence. At this point my advice is to move straight onto the next exercise. Do not start to ponder what you have not had a chance to say during the five minutes. It is time to move on. You cannot change what has already happened.

End of activity phase
When the buzzer sounds at the end of your last exercise the assessor will tell you that your assessment centre is over and ask you to leave the room and proceed to the assessment centre corridor. Leave the booklet on the desk and collect all your belongings. Do not enter into a conversation with the role actor or assessor. The role actor will drop their head as they are still in role and the assessor has to complete your assessment by calculating your grades for each of the competency areas.

Debrief
Once out in the assessment centre corridor you will be directed towards the candidate co-ordinator. Do not forget you are still under assessment centre conditions so do not talk as you leave the corridor. The candidate co-ordinator will then take you to the cloakroom for a short debrief and to collect your personal belongings. The debrief is the time to raise any issues you feel may have had an effect on your performance. If you do need to do this, the candidate co-ordinator will speak to you in private. If you do this, you must follow the rules and submit your appeal within seven days.

Divisional Profile

You should receive this document about six weeks before your assessment centre date. Its purpose is to provide you with background to your role as a sergeant or inspector in the force and division in which the actual assessment centre is located. It will contain management information and structure of the division and, if you are undertaking the sergeant assessment centre, details of your team.

The profile will also contain force policies. Read and familiarise yourself with these policies as any policies used in the profile will be reproduced in the exercise candidate information. Consequently, you will recognise the policy and be able to double check it to ensure the content is the same and also making any notes you wish to use in your interaction with the role actor. You do not need to know any policies from your own force extensively. The Part II assessment centre is not based in your own force and it is not a test of your knowledge of your own force policies or procedures.

When you receive the divisional profile you will also receive a letter that lists the names of the exercises and a brief description as to the content of the exercise. For example:

Todd: in this exercise you will meet a member of the public to discuss a community issue.

Do not use this list in conjunction with the divisional profile to try and pre-empt the content of the exercises. Your idea of the content of the exercises may be far removed from the actual exercise. Consequently, your idea of how to deal with the actual exercise will be affected. Similarly do not listen or be guided by those individuals who claim to know what the exercises will contain by reviewing the name and content of the exercises in conjunction with the divisional profile. Only the exercise design team has this information.

Contamination

This is the term used to describe an instance when a candidate is aware of the exercise content. It is very tempting to want to know what the exercise content is but I would strongly warn you against it.

Candidates usually find out the exercise content from a friend or colleague who has already attended the Part II assessment centre. When you have completed the exercises in this book ask yourself one question; could you recall every word of the candidate information in all seven exercises and every response a role actor gave in all seven exercises? If you become contaminated, you will have some idea of the exercise candidate information content and the role actor lines. Consequently, candidates do not then ask relevant questions as their friend or colleague has provided them with the information. Those questions may be on the assessment checklist. If the candidate *states* the information to the role actor and does not *ask* the role actor for the information, they will not score the behavioural statement that relate to the question.

A colleague or friend's interpretation of the exercise may not be the correct one. It has been proven that contamination is a hindrance, not an assistance. You will go into the exercises with preconceived ideas of what you think you need to do and more than likely this will not be beneficial to you.

No doubt you will meet someone who will tell you they passed having known all of the exercises and what they were about. These people are the exception rather than the rule. I suspect their success may be contributable to their assessment centre preparation rather than that they knew the content of the exercises.

It is also worth bearing in mind that passing information about the exercises to another party is a breach of the Code of Conduct. The content of the exercises is confidential information and should be treated in the same way as you treat confidential information you come across in your day-to-day duties.

It has been shown on more than one occasion that contamination does not work. If it did wouldn't everyone pass?

This book contains a total of 14 exercises. Seven have been designed to relate to the rank of sergeant and seven to the rank of inspector. Both sets of seven comprise of four police exercises (where you will have to deal with a member of the police organisation) and three non-police exercises (where you will have to deal with a member of the public). This ratio reflects the traditional ratio found in a Part II assessment centre.

Each exercise comprises three parts:

- Candidate information (this is the information you read during your preparation phase) followed by a candidate information debrief.
- Role actor instructions (containing background, prompts and responses) followed by a role actor instructions debrief.
- Assessment checklist (compiled to reflect a Part II assessment checklist in terms of number of competency areas and behavioural statements) followed by an assessment checklist debrief.

When reading through the candidate information consider the following questions and make your notes accordingly:

- What is this exercise about?
- What do you consider to be the key issues in the exercise?
- What would a good candidate do or ask?
- What do you need to clarify?
- How would you address the issues you consider relevant?

First, study the candidate information and make notes of the points you want to raise or clarify with the role actor. Resist the temptation to read the role actor instructions or the assessment checklist before you have made your notes. There is no point in cheating yourself.

Here are some tips for working through the exercise. They are the methods I employed when undertaking both my sergeant and inspector Part II, however, they are only tips and you should use whatever method you are comfortable with.

- Making short prompts to follow will give you sufficient direction to the key points in your notes. Use a highlighter pen to indicate the points you want to raise with the role actor. Try indicating a positive piece of performance with the note '+ve' or simply write 'mention'. Similarly, to draw your attention to under performance write '-ve' or again 'mention'.

- Make your notes on the actual document itself. Candidates sometimes make their notes on the rear of the exercise front cover. This then restricts them to just referring to this one sheet during their interaction with the role actor. It may be to your advantage to flick from one page of the candidate information to the other during your interaction with the role actor as your eye may be drawn to something you would otherwise have missed.

- You do not have to follow a rigid set structure when dealing with the role actor, nor is there any requirement to re-write the candidate information.

- When using the exercises in this book, read your first exercise without putting yourself under the time constraints of the Part II assessment centre. Familiarise yourself with the exercise format first then introduce the time constraints. You should allow yourself six minutes preparation time per exercise.

- Once you have undertaken the exercises individually try completing all seven within the total time allowed in the assessment centre. Allow yourself 45 minutes. As with the assessment centre, after 43 minutes have elapsed, check your progress. This will be the point at which the assessment centre buzzer will sound to warn you that in two minutes the first role actor and assessor will be entering the room.

- To assist you in undertaking the above, take a gummed notelet and attach it to the front cover of each of the seven exercises. That way you will not waste valuable time leafing through the book to find the start of each exercise.

- To further enhance your appreciation of the assessment centre time constraints try practising with the seven exercises in the book not relevant to the rank you are preparing for. If nothing else it will give you extra practice experiencing the time constraints.

Although you may not think so, the front cover of any exercise contains important information for you. The name of the exercise is always the name of the role actor you will be meeting. On occasion candidates have become confused as to who they will be meeting, especially when an exercise may contain three or four names.

The line outlining the number of pages contained within the material is also important to you. Ensure that you read all the documents contained in an exercise and remember that no one piece of candidate information carries more weight or importance than any other.

Finally, a line confirms the person you will be meeting in the activity phase of the exercise.

The memorandums, e-mails and letters contained in the candidate information are addressed to Sergeant 'Candidate', Team 5, Castleside. It would be a very time consuming task for the team responsible for delivering the assessment centre to personally address all documents using candidates' actual names hence the use of Sergeant 'Candidate'.

Similarly the date shown on documents will not show a specific date but will say 'yesterday' or 'two days ago' or whenever the facts relating to the documents have occurred.

Candidate instructions

In this exercise you will receive two pages of preparatory information:

- a memorandum from Sergeant Weller
- a copy of an e-mail from Constable White

During the activity phase you will meet Constable A Butler.

RESTRICTED

CASTLESHIRE
POLICE

CASTLESHIRE POLICE

Memorandum

From:	Sergeant Weller
To:	Sergeant 'Candidate', Team 5, Castleside
Subject:	Constable Butler
Date:	yesterday

I have just received the attached e-mail from Constable Alan White, who is a student officer. Constable White has been on the team for six weeks and I thought he was settling in well to the role and as part of the team. He is a mature entrant having previously worked as a teacher. He is currently being tutored by Constable Butler.

Constable Butler has five years' service and in the two years under my supervision, the officer has always been extremely professional and is well respected by colleagues. As an experienced tutor, Constable Butler's case files have always been to the highest standards and are an example to other members of the team. For your information, three months ago, Constable Butler was the driver of a vehicle when it struck a kerb causing damage to a wheel. However, I am not aware of any incidents prior to this and generally would be out of character for Constable Butler.

The matters raised in the e-mail are an obvious cause for concern and I would have liked to have dealt with this matter myself. Unfortunately, I was not working nights as I was at headquarters and as both Constable White and Constable Butler are on football duty today, I have not had the opportunity to speak directly to either officer. I have, therefore, arranged for Constable Butler to see you on your first day.

J Weller

Sergeant

RESTRICTED
Email Printout

From:	Constable White, Team 5
To:	Sergeant Weller, Team 5
Date:	yesterday
Subject:	Constable Butler
Security:	RESTRICTED

Sergeant,

I'm sorry to have to bring this to your attention and really wanted to speak to you in person. I appreciate I have only been with the team for six weeks and I believe I have fitted in well and benefited from Constable Butler's experience. However, as I have tried to deal with this matter myself to no avail, I feel it necessary to inform you of the following incidents, both of which occurred last week.

Firstly, on Tuesday night, there was an alarm activation at Atkins Jewellers. We were about a mile away and as we turned into the High Street from Eastfield Road, the car was travelling so fast that it skidded when taking the corner. I did not feel Constable Butler was in full control and I also saw two pedestrians who were on the pavement looked quite startled. Whilst we were waiting for the key holder I said to Constable Butler that I thought we were lucky and nearly lost it on the corner. This comment was just laughed off.

The second incident, on Thursday night, occurred when we were responding to a call of a fight outside Castle's Kebabs, Moat Street. We had the two tones and blue light on, but Constable Butler was driving so fast that as we entered the Prince's Way roundabout, even though there is a restricted view, we didn't slow down at all. Fortunately, there was no other traffic but I feel the driving was beyond Constable Butler's ability. I again tried to speak with Constable Butler, but my comments were just dismissed, calling me a 'stupid pratt' and saying I should keep my comments to myself, as I am not a police trained driver.

On both occasions Constable Stewart was acting sergeant and as she is a friend of Constable Butler, I didn't feel it appropriate to speak with her. I do not want to make an official complaint, but I do want this resolved so I can concentrate on learning the job.

Alan White
Constable

Candidate information debrief

Memorandum from Sergeant Weller:

The opening paragraph of Sergeant Weller's memorandum provides you with some facts relating to Constable White, a student officer (formally known as probationer constables). Constable White has only been on team 5 for six weeks and is being tutored by Constable Butler, the officer you will be meeting. Significantly, Sergeant Weller states in the second sentence 'and I thought he was settling in well'. Did you identify this as a potential indication as to any issues in the exercise? I would always urge caution at trying to pre-empt or second guess what an exercise may be about before you have read all the candidate information.

The second paragraph of the memorandum provides you with information relating to Constable Butler. No doubt you will have identified that Constable Butler has always conducted him/herself in a professional manner, is well respected by colleagues and, his/her case files have been of the highest standard. All these are positive points you may want to raise during your meeting with the officer. But, once again, do not try and second guess what the exercise issues may be.

The memorandum then gives you details of an incident that occurred three months ago whilst Constable Butler was driving a police vehicle. There were no incidents prior to this and Sergeant Weller states the incident was out of character for Constable Butler. As a candidate, there are a number of facts that require clarification, namely what was the result of the incident three months previously? Why is this out of character?

Finally, the memorandum outlines that the email from Constable White does give cause for concern. However, Sergeant Weller has been unable to speak with either officer. So it is over to you to deal with the matters raised.

E-mail from Constable White:

The opening paragraph outlines that Constable White has benefited from Constable Butler's experience. Once again, a positive comment in favour of Constable Butler and one you may be able to use during your interaction. Constable White then goes on to outline two incidents, both of which occurred the previous week.

Perhaps you identified a number of issues contained in the description of the incidents that requires you to seek further clarification.

For example, what caused the incidents to occur, further details of the incidents, did Constable Butler call Constable White a 'stupid pratt'? I will refer to these issues in more depth when we review the assessment checklist.

Finally, the e-mail outlines that Constable White does not want to make a complaint regarding Constable Butler's behaviour. However, during your interaction with Constable Butler you could mention this as a potential personal consequence of his actions.

Role actor instructions

As you read through the role actor instructions consider the following questions and make your notes accordingly:

- How would a good candidate react to the replies given by Butler?
- Has the exercise changed? If so what do you now consider to be the issues contained in the exercise?

You are Andrew/Andrea Butler. You are single and have five years' service, which has all been at Castleside. You are a tutor constable and for the past six weeks have been tutoring Constable Alan White, the third officer you have tutored this year. You have attended driving courses during your probation and consider yourself to be a competent and confident driver.

Overall, you have been getting on very well with Constable White and you have been impressed with the enthusiasm shown in getting to grips with the role. However, during a night shift last week, there were two occasions when Constable White criticised your driving, you believe unjustly. The first incident occurred on Tuesday night when you were responding to an alarm activation at Atkins Jewellers. As you turned into the High Street from Eastfield Road, the car skidded as you took the corner. Two pedestrians were at the side of the road and looked quite startled as you drove past. When Constable White stated you were lucky and nearly lost it on the corner, you just laughed it off. The second incident occurred on Thursday night when responding to a report of a fight outside Castle's Kebabs, Moat Street. You were using the two tones and blue light, but 'chanced' the roundabout maintaining your speed as you entered the Prince's Way roundabout. Fortunately, even though there is a restricted view, there was no other traffic about. When Constable White spoke to you about your driving, you called him a 'stupid pratt' saying he should keep his comments to himself as he is not a police trained driver.

Three months ago, you were given words of advice from Inspector Noon for damaging a vehicle when you struck a kerb on the way to a report of a violent domestic dispute. Recently, you have had a tendency to concentrate on getting to incidents quickly, in the process shutting everything else out. Constable White is your third consecutive student officer back to back and you could do with a break. You do want to continue in the role long term. You are well respected and your paperwork is held as an example to others on your team.

Demeanour: confident.

When you enter the room, say:

1. "Hello Sergeant, I'm Andy/Andrea Butler. Sergeant Weller left me a note to come and see you."

   If the candidate asks how you feel about tutoring, say:

2. "It's hard work at times and there is the extra responsibility to consider."

   If the candidate asks how you are getting on with Constable White, say:

3. "Overall fine. He seems to have a good grasp of the basics and is keen to learn."

   If the candidate asks about the incident of skidding when responding to the alarm, say:

4. "I don't know what all the fuss is about. I've been driving marked vehicles for the past five years. Perhaps when he attends a course he might come to his senses."

   If the candidate points out that the reaction of the two pedestrians, say:

5. "I was concentrating on the road and they were on the pavement well out of the way."

   If the candidate asks about the roundabout incident when responding to the fight, say:

6. "That was so minor I can hardly remember it. There was no other traffic and no one was put in danger."

   If the candidate asks if you called Constable White a 'stupid pratt', say:

7. "I probably did, but he was being pathetic and would have been better off concentrating on the job in hand."

   If the candidate asks about the incident when you struck the kerb, say:

8. "That was unfortunate. I just clipped the kerb. No one was injured."

   If the candidate asks why these incidents have occurred, say:

9 "At times I just tend to shut everything else out and concentrate on getting to the call quickly."

If the candidate states you were lucky/need to be more careful/have a responsibility to set an example, say:

10 "I understand what you are saying."

If the candidate suggests that you need to calm down or consider safety issues, say:

11 "I suppose you've got a point. But it can be tiring always having to think for someone else as well."

If the candidate asks if you would like a break from tutoring, say:

12 "That's something to think about and perhaps concentrate on myself."

If the candidate highlights positive comments from Sergeant Weller, say:

13 "Thanks Sergeant. I take pride in my paperwork and always want to perform to the best of my ability."

If the candidate suggests meeting with or apologising to Constable White, say:

14 "He's been a bit off lately. I suppose that might help."

Role actor instructions debrief

As you will have noticed, the exercise is not gender specific, a male or female role actor can undertake the role of Constable Butler. Remember the gender or ethnicity of a role actor should not influence the way you deal with an exercise. Should the gender or ethnicity be an issue, this will be apparent in the candidate information.

Constable Butler has five years police service. Constable White is the third officer to have been tutored by Constable Butler this year. Generally Constable Butler's relationship with White is good.

The role actor instructions then give details of the two driving incidents and Butler's actions during the incidents. You will have no doubt identified that this is the same information that appears in the candidate information. It is essential that the role actor receives the same information. If this were not the case then the consistency would be lost from the exercise delivery and candidates would be disadvantaged.

The role actor instructions then provide information relating to the incident three months ago when Constable Butler struck a kerb. On this occasion Constable Butler received words of advice from Inspector Noon. Perhaps you consider Constable Butler's driving to be one of the issues contained within the exercise and would seek to pursue this during your meeting. Should you do this the role actor would provide you with the details of their meeting with Inspector Noon and the way in which Inspector Noon dealt with the matter.

Significantly, the role actor instructions inform you that Constable Butler feels they could do with a break from tutoring student officers. This would be for you to deal with, as Constable Butler's line manager.

Role actor response 1 of the role actor script does not provide you with any significant information other than the role actor confirming their identity and that they were asked to see you by Sergeant Weller. Always allow the role actor the opportunity to deliver their opening line. It assists you to confirm their identity and they may say something to which you have to respond.

Role actor response 2 suggests that perhaps Constable Butler would prefer a break from tutoring. Should you wish to pursue this further, the role actor would use the information contained in the role actor instructions that relates to wanting to take a break. It would then be up to you to respond accordingly.

Role actor response 3 provides you with the information that

Constable Butler's relationship with Constable White is not a major issue. There is no ill feeling between the two officers and Constable Butler has been impressed by Constable White's attitude.

Role actor response 4 certainly would require a response from you. Constable Butler's attitude does need addressing. However, remember to stay within the bounds of the Respect for Race and Diversity competency area. Candidates sometimes wrongly believe that they should address a person's performance by being very forthright. This could be reflected in your Respect for Race and Diversity grade. I will refer to this further when we debrief the assessment checklist.

Role actor response 5 would lead you to outlining the consequences of driving in such a manner or the perception that members of the public would have, should they witness such an incident.

Role actor response 6 is similar to reply 5 in that you need to address the attitude of Constable Butler and outline the consequences of driving in such a manner.

Role actor response 7 also gives you the opportunity to address Constable Butler's attitude. Significantly, it also provides you with the opportunity to outline the affect such actions have on Constable White.

Role actor response 8 refers to the incident three months before when Constable Butler struck the kerb. Once again, you may feel that you need to address the attitude in much the same way as you did to role actor response 5.

Role actor response 9 is certainly worthy of a response by you. You should address this by outlining the potential consequences of driving in such a manner.

Role actor response 10 is not confrontational and Constable Butler does not object to any suggestions that may fall within the remit of the specific reply prompt.

Role actor response 11 is similar to reply 10 but has the added information of Constable Butler stating, 'it can be tiring having to think for someone else as well'. Again, you should respond to this by merely clarifying what he/she means by this. That would then bring out Constable Butler's views on carrying on as a tutor.

Role actor response 12 outlines Constable Butler's response to the suggestion that they have a break from tutoring. You could respond to this by offering your support or suggestions to assist Constable Butler.

Role actor response 13 is a response to you having identified the positive comments from Sergeant Weller's memorandum. As you will discover when we debrief the assessment checklist this will benefit you in not only in a specific competency area but also in Respect for Race and Diversity.

Role actor response 14 again suggests that there is no animosity between Constables Butler and White.

Notice that throughout the role actor lines whenever you suggest an option you will not receive replies along the lines of, 'What a good idea Sergeant' or 'That sounds as if it would work'. For who can say if one suggestion is any better than another? If it falls within the parameters of a specific behavioural statement, then that will suffice.

The role actor will not use all the responses they have in a script. They will only use the reply specific to a prompt and will not force a reply into the conversation if it does not warrant it, as this may disadvantage a candidate.

Assessment checklist

Competency Area	Scalar	Grade

Area 1: Effective Communication

Asks role actor:

Thorough – Superficial

1 2 3 4 5   A B C D

1.1 for views on role as tutor constable
1.2 if wishes to continue as tutor constable
1.3 for details of kerbing incident
1.4 for reasons incidents have occurred
1.5 if called officer a 'stupid pratt'
1.6 for details of previous conversation with
     Insp Noon

Area 2: Maximising Potential

Acknowledges:

Thorough – Superficial

1 2 3 4 5   A B C D

2.1 role actor's past performance/experience
2.2 role of tutor/responsibilities/role model
2.3 Encourages role actor to continue tutoring
     Constable White
2.4 Suggests role actor has break from
     tutoring after Constable White

Area 3: Resilience

Informs role actor:

Clear – Unclear

1 2 3 4 5   A B C D

3.1 that comments are unacceptable
3.2 will speak to Constable White
3.3 will monitor future conduct/driving

Explains consequences:

3.4 of driving incidents (e.g. offences/collisions/
     public perception)
3.5 of treatment of White (e.g. loss confidence/
     loss respect as tutor)

Area 4: Respect for Race and Diversity

Objective – Biased   A B C D

1 2 3 4 5

Supportive – Unsupportive

1 2 3 4 5

Assessment checklist debrief

As you can see the Butler exercise contains four competency areas; Effective Communication, Maximising Potential, Resilience and Respect for Race and Diversity.

Overall the exercise contains 15 behavioural statements (statements a candidate should say). Remember there will be no more than six and no less than three behavioural statements in a competency area. Respect for Race and Diversity does not contain behavioural statements.

To debrief each competency area and behavioural statement in turn, have your candidate information and role actor notes to hand to see which behavioural statements you would have scored.

Area 1: Effective Communication

This area contains the maximum six behavioural statements. Notice that all are prefixed by 'Asks role actor'. The scalar (how a candidate scores the behavioural statements) for this area is Thorough to Superficial.

1.1 ... for views on role as tutor constable. This can be identified from the candidate information. There is an indication in Sergeant Weller's memorandum and Constable White's e-mail that Constable Butler may not be content with the role as a tutor constable. Asking this question would elicit role actor response 2 of the role actor script.

1.2 ... if wishes to continue as tutor constable. A perfectly legitimate question to ask. Perhaps you may consider that Constable Butler would benefit from a break in tutoring student officers. This question would result in receiving role actor response 12.

1.3 ... for details of kerbing incident. This question could be asked if you are trying to establish a pattern to Constable Butler's driving. After all, you have the kerb incident three months ago and the two incidents outlined in Constable White's e-mail.

1.4 ... for reasons incidents have occurred. This is a key question. You will have no doubt identified that something has resulted in a change of behaviour/attitude in recent months. There is a clear indication of this at the end of paragraph two in Sergeant Weller's memorandum.

1.5 ... if called officer a 'stupid pratt'. Confirming that this comment was passed will lead you onto addressing it and the subsequent effect.

1.6 ... for details of previous conversation with Insp. Noon.
Perhaps you need to be aware as to how Constable Butler was dealt with
in relation to the kerbing incident by Inspector Noon. The Inspector may
have imposed driving restrictions on Constable Butler. You need to be aware
of this as it will provide you with important information and help you deal
with the recent driving incidents mentioned by Constable White.

Area 2: Maximising Potential

This area contains four behavioural statements. Notice that the first two
are prefixed by 'Acknowledges'. The scalar (how a candidate scores the
behavioural statements) for this area is Thorough to Superficial.

2.1 ... role actor's past performance/experience. I mentioned when
debriefing the candidate information and role actor instructions that it is
important to not merely focus on the negative aspects of a persons
performance. This behavioural statement shows that you should also
acknowledge the positive aspects of Constable Butler's behaviour, such as
that outlined in Sergeant Weller's memorandum.

2.2 ... role of tutor/responsibilities/role model. By responding
sympathetically to role actor responses 2 or 12 you would cover this
behavioural statement as would acknowledging their role from details
given in the candidate information.

**2.3 ... Encourages role actor to continue tutoring Constable
White.** Constable White clearly states in the e-mail to have benefited
from Constable White's experience. To remove Constable Butler as tutor
constable may have a detrimental affect on Constable White's
development. The partnership should continue with future monitoring
by you (behavioural statement 3.3).

**2.4 ... Suggests role actor has break from tutoring after
Constable White.** Conversely you have a responsibility for Constable
Butler's welfare. As Constable Butler has indicated he/she does feel the
need for a break from tutoring duties and responsibilities.

Area 3: Resilience

This area contains five behavioural statements. Notice that the first three
are prefixed by 'Informs role actor' and the last two by 'Explains
consequences'. The scalar (how a candidate scores the behavioural
statements) for this area is Clear to Unclear.

3.1 ...that comments are unacceptable. This behavioural statement could follow on from 1.5. Having confirmed that Constable Butler made the comment, you then need to address it.

3.2 ...will speak to Constable White. Constable White obviously feels so strongly about the way he has been treated by Constable Butler and the driving incidents that he has felt the need to bring it to the attention of the team sergeant. Consequently you need to speak to the officer. This may be to obtain further information or to inform them that their concerns have been addressed. If you state you will speak to Constable White you would score the behavioural statement but if you also state the reason why you intend to do so you would move up the scalar for this behavioural statement.

3.3 ... will monitor future conduct/driving. You are the team sergeant and monitoring Constable Butler's conduct and/or driving should be part of your responsibilities.

3.4 ... of driving incidents. When interacting with the role actor ensure that you explain the consequences – it is not enough to simply ask the role actor if they know what the consequences are. The driving incidents outlined by Constable White certainly require addressing. Explaining the consequences reinforces the importance of maintaining driving standards.

3.5 ... of treatment of White. Similar to 3.4, Constable White is a student officer and the effect of Constable Butler's treatment could have a serious effect on him both personally and professionally.

Area 4: Respect for Race and Diversity
As I previously mentioned, this competency area does not contain behavioural statements. You are assessed across the five-minute interaction against two scalars, in this case Objective to Biased and Supportive – Unsupportive.

You should maintain a balanced view when dealing with the exercises. If you focus on the negative aspects, such as under per-formance, you would miss offering your support to Constable Butler, which would affect your grade for Respect for Race and Diversity.

Ho

Candidate instructions

In this exercise you will receive four pages of preparatory information:

- a memorandum from Sergeant Weller
- a memorandum from M Sidhu, File Checking Unit (three pages)

During the activity phase you will meet Constable G Ho.

CASTLESHIRE POLICE

Memorandum

From:	Sergeant Weller
To:	Sergeant 'Candidate', Team 5, Castleside
Subject:	Constable Ho
Date:	yesterday

Please see the attached memorandum from M Sidhu, Castleside File Checking Unit, incorporating the performance figures for team 5.

I feel the team has been let down by the fact Mr Sidhu has had to submit the comments in his report, particularly as the incident involving Constable Ho was reported in the Castleside Gazette and they were keen to follow the case through to court.

Overall, the team has been performing well, apart from Constable Ho. Constable Ho has four years' service and is well known and respected within the community, having lived in the area all their life. The officer has made some notable arrests for robbery following an operation six months ago and did have aspirations for CID.

As I have not been able to speak to the officer myself, I have asked Constable Ho to meet with you on your first day.

J Weller

Sergeant

CASTLESHIRE POLICE

Memorandum

From:	M Sidhu, File Checking Unit
To:	Sergeant Weller, team 5, Castleside
Subject:	*R v Paul Kennedy* – no evidence offered and team 5 performance figures
Date:	3 days ago

I am disappointed to have to inform that in the criminal damage case of *R v Paul Kennedy*, we have been forced to offer no evidence. The reasons for this are due to the fact that we only received the file from Constable Ho three days ago and that a critical witness statement had not been obtained.

Whilst the enquiry officers tried to speak to the witness, they were unable to do so due to the fact that the mobile phone number had been incorrectly written down.

Please find attached the statistics for team 5 in relation to the last three months in respect of number of files submitted, percentage timeliness and sufficient to proceed.

M Sidhu

Unit Head

Team 5 performance figures – second quarter

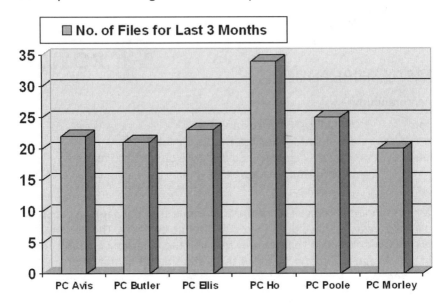

Chart 1 – Divisional average 21 files per officer

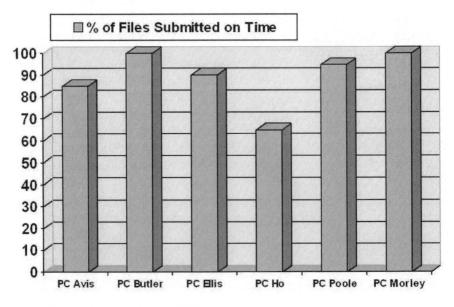

Chart 2 – Divisional Target 80%

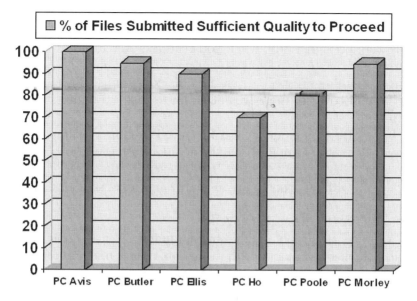

Chart 3– Divisional Target 80%

Candidate information debrief

What were your thoughts when you read the exercise front cover and saw that you had to read four pages of preparatory information? Perhaps it was a daunting prospect, given the time constraints. However, as you have now discovered, there was not a lot to read contained within the four pages.

I have tried to include, across the seven exercises, examples of the different types and formats of candidate information you may receive at your Part 2 assessment centre. In this exercise the basic charts will provide you with an opportunity to analyse figures or statistics.

Memorandum from Sergeant Weller

The second paragraph of the memorandum clearly indicates that Sergeant Weller is unhappy with the action, or lack of action, relating to a matter concerning Constable Ho. You would not be wrong to assume in this exercise that Constable Ho has failed in his duties relating to file submission or preparation. This is obvious as the author of the other memorandum is from the File Checking Unit. Clearly an article regarding a case involving Constable Ho has been reported in the local press.

Sergeant Weller's memorandum then goes on to explain that Constable Ho is not performing as well as the other team 5 members. The memorandum then contains a positive comment in relation to Constable Ho's relationship with the community. Significantly, the officer has had some notable arrests for robbery and had aspirations to join the CID. Is this information significant given the issues relating to files? Is Constable Ho taking on too much work?

Memorandum from M Sidhu

As you can see, the memorandum refers to two issues; a case concerning a defendant called Paul Kennedy and the team 5 performance figures. Did you consider there might be a link between these two issues?

The first paragraph clarifies what Sergeant Weller's concerns were as referred to in their memorandum. It would appear that the case against Paul Kennedy has folded as no evidence could to be offered. The person responsible for this is Constable Ho who submitted the file late and without a crucial witness statement.

To make matters worse, the File Checking Unit enquiry clerks were unable to trace the witness as Constable Ho had written their telephone number down incorrectly. Obviously you will have realised by now that you have a number of issues to raise when you meet Constable Ho.

The last paragraph in the memorandum directs you to the statistics from the File Checking Unit.

Did you find the statistics easy to use? The charts are quite basic and Constable Ho's performance in the three categories can be easily identified. The charts will be covered in greater detail in the assessment checklist debrief.

No doubt you will have a number of queries which you will want to clarify, particularly relating to why Constable Ho has been performing in such a manner, and there is only one person who can answer those queries – your other source of information in an exercise: the role actor.

Role actor instructions

You are Gavin/Glenda Ho. You have four years' service, which has all been spent at Castleside. You enjoy your role and having lived in the area all your life, have used your local knowledge to best effect and established a good reputation within the community.

Two weeks ago you arrested Paul Kennedy for criminal damage at Castleside Cricket Club, where a number of windows were smashed. You were late submitting the case papers due to your overall workload. Additionally, you were unable to obtain a witness statement and had hoped the enquiry officers at the File Checking Unit would do so. You are unaware that you had recorded the witness' mobile telephone number incorrectly. Due to the number of recent incidents at the cricket club, the Castleside Gazette reported the arrest of Paul Kennedy and were keen to follow the case through to its conclusion at court.

You are unaware of the reason why you have been asked to see the new team sergeant or of the report from the File Checking Unit. Within the team, you have a much higher than average arrest rate, but this has affected your efficiency, and the quality of your files and timeliness of submissions is suffering as a consequence. Six months ago you organised an operation that resulted in the arrest of three separate street robbery suspects. As a result of this, you informed Sergeant Weller at your last performance review of your interest in applying for the CID.

Demeanour: confident

When you enter the room, say:

1.   **"Hello Sergeant I'm Gavin/Glenda Ho. I was sent an e-mail by Sergeant Weller to come and see you."**

If the candidate asks if you know what the meeting is about, say:

2.   **"No. I thought it was the usual welcome and introductory chat."**

If the candidate asks about the criminal damage arrest, say:

3.   **"I was in the area when a local resident stopped me and said they'd just seen a youth smashing windows at the cricket club. I arrested Paul Kennedy after a short chase in the grounds."**

If the candidate asks why you didn't obtain the witness statement, say:

4. "The witness wasn't available at the time and I had to process Paul. I just haven't had a chance since."

If the candidate asks why the case papers were submitted late, say:

5. "I've been really busy and it slipped my mind. I still got the papers to the File Checking Unit three days before the court date."

If the candidate informs you that the witness' mobile phone number was incorrect, say:

6. "I didn't know that but that's an easy mistake to make. They were in a hurry at the time and I just wrote the details down quickly."

If the candidate outlines the consequences of poor file submissions or the need to concentrate on quality as opposed to quantity, say:

7. "I take your point but I've always tried to maintain a high arrest rate."

If the candidate asks for details about the robbery operation, say:

8. "I did some plain clothes work in the town centre following some street robberies involving mobile phones. We struck lucky and arrested a couple of local youths on two separate occasions"

If the candidate suggests ways to improve your time management or handling workload, say:

9. "If you think that will help, I'll give it a go."

If the candidate asks about your career aspirations, say:

10. "I would like to get on the CID and I thought getting the arrests was the best way of getting noticed."

If the candidate asks about your current workload, say:

11. "I have about five files live at the moment."

Role actor instructions debrief

The first thing that is apparent with the Ho exercise is that it is not gender specific. Ho has four years police service, all of which has been spent at Castleside. The officer enjoys their role and has used their knowledge of the area to a positive effect in their role. They have also established a good reputation within the community. This information is contained in Sergeant Weller's memorandum and is perhaps information you feel you may want to use during the interaction with Ho.

It is this type of information you should identify in documents to use in your interaction with the role actor, even if you may only consider this information as minor background details. I always feel in exercises where the issues relate to an officer under performing that it is worthwhile considering how you would like to be treated in those circumstances. As a candidate you obviously need to address the under performance but you can do this in a way that is not insensitive, biased or overbearing.

The role actor instructions go on to provide details of the incident involving Paul Kennedy and the damage to the cricket club windows.

You will have noticed that each of the role actor instructions contained in the book has a demeanour that the role actor must follow. This is included to ensure consistency in the delivery of the exercise by the role actor and to ensure fairness to all candidates.

Role actor response 1 confirms the role actor's identity and that they were asked to come and meet you.

Role actor response 2 confirms that Ho is unaware as to the reason for the meeting. Consequently this should indicate to you to get on with addressing those issues.

Role actor response 3 provides you with details of the Paul Kennedy arrest. This point will be covered in more detail in the assessment checklist debrief.

Role actor response 4 provides you with the reason as to why the key witness statement wasn't obtained. How would you react to this response? The final part of the response would tend to suggest that Ho has a heavy workload. Is this the case? If so how are you, as their line manager, going to address it?

Role actor response 5 is similar to 4 in that it suggests that Ho has been busy. Ho's attitude relating to the file submission needs to be addressed. Obviously, in this instance it left the File Checking Unit staff little time in which to obtain the witness statement.

Role actor response 6 also suggests that the quality of Ho's work is being compromised in favour of expediency. You may feel that this is something you want to address.

Role actor response 7 outlines Ho's views towards their workload. How would you respond to this response? The fact that they try to maintain a high arrest rate is commendable but this needs to be balanced with quality investigations and file submissions.

Role actor response 8 refers to the robbery operation which is mentioned in Sergeant Weller's memorandum. This will be covered in more detail in the assessment checklist debrief.

Role actor response 9 is a standard Part 2 assessment centre response. As I mentioned previously, the role actor will not reply with such platitudes as, 'What an excellent idea. I'll give it a go' or 'That really is a good idea and worth trying'.

Role actor response 10 outlines Ho's future career aspirations. How would you respond to the fact that they consider getting arrests is the best way to get noticed? Perhaps it relates to the quality and quantity issues. I cannot emphasise enough the need to use, listen and respond to the role actors.

Role actor response 11 is a key fact for you to consider. This may be your first question to Ho as you have identified that Ho is making a number of errors in their work and, quite rightly, you want to explore the reasons why this is the case.

Assessment checklist

Competency Area	Scalar	Grade

Area 1: Effective Communication
Asks role actor:

Scalar: Thorough – Superficial 1 2 3 4 5 — Grade: A B C D

1.1 for details about criminal damage arrest
1.2 for details about robbery operation
1.3 about current workload
1.4 about their career aspirations
1.5 why witness statement was not obtained

Area 2: Maximising Potential
Explains charts regarding:

Scalar: Thorough – Superficial 1 2 3 4 5 — Grade: A B C D

2.1 number of files submitted
2.2 files submitted on time
2.3 files sufficient quality to proceed
2.4 Acknowledges role actor's experience/ arrests
2.5 Outlines need to balance arrests/ investigations

Area 3: Problem Solving
Suggests:

Scalar: Clear – Unclear 1 2 3 4 5 — Grade: A B C D

3.1 attachment to the File Checking Unit
3.2 methods to manage files/workload
3.3 Offers self as support
3.4 Informs role actor will monitor future workload

Area 4: Resilience

Scalar: Clear – Unclear 1 2 3 4 5 — Grade: A B C D

4.1 Informs role actor that phone number was incorrect

Outlines consequences:
4.2 of poor quality/late submission of files
4.3 of discontinuance of Kennedy case

Area 5: Respect for Race and Diversity

Constructive – Dismissive 1 2 3 4 5   A B C D
Supportive – Unsupportive 1 2 3 4 5

Ho assessment checklist debrief

As you can see, the Ho exercise contains the maximum five competency areas; Effective Communication, Maximising Potential, Problem Solving, Resilience and Respect for Race and Diversity.

The exercise contains 17 behavioural statements (statements a candidate should say).

Have your candidate information and role actor notes to hand to see which behavioural statements you would have scored.

Area 1: Effective Communication

This area contains five behavioural statements. Notice that all are prefixed by 'Asks role actor'. The scalar (how well a candidate scores the behavioural statements) for this area is Thorough to Superficial.

1.1 ... for details about criminal damage arrest. I referred to this incident in the role actor instructions (role actor response 3). As Ho's new line manager you are unaware of the arrest involving Kennedy and may feel that this information may help you build up a picture of the case. It does state in Sergeant Weller's memorandum that the local press were following the case.

1.2 ... for details about robbery operation. The robbery operation is referred to in Sergeant Weller's memorandum. It is clear from this information that Ho has had a notable success with the operation and this is certainly worthy of acknowledgement by you.

1.3 ... about current workload. This question would produce role actor response 11. As the line manager it is essential that you build up a picture of Ho's workload, as this may be an issue you need to address.

1.4 ... about their career aspirations. Sergeant Weller in their memorandum states that Ho did have aspirations to join the CID. Is this still the case? Asking this question would result in the delivery of role actor response 10. You would then need to address that response.

1.5 ... why witness statement was not obtained. The case against Paul Kennedy has collapsed because a witness statement was not obtained. As Ho's line manager you need to know why this is the case. This question would result in role actor response 4.

Area 2: Maximising Potential

This area contains five behavioural statements. Notice that the first three are prefixed by 'Explains charts regarding'. The scalar for this area is Thorough to Superficial.

I will deal with behavioural statements 2.1 (**... number of files submitted**), 2.2 (**... files submitted on time**) and 2.3 (**... files sufficient quality to proceed**) together as all three charts and the information they contain is similar. Note that the scalar for this competency area is Thorough to Superficial.

When using charts in an exercise, particularly in this instance where the exercise contains more than one, always ensure that you mention which chart you are referring to. That way the assessor will be aware and will therefore be able to assess you accordingly.

It is clear that Ho has the highest number of file submissions in the past three months but is lowest for files submitted on time and sufficient quality to proceed. They are also below the divisional target of 80 per cent.

Let us use the chart relating to files submitted on time as the example of how you can score using charts. If you say to Ho during your interaction, 'You have the lowest number of files submitted on time', this would score behavioural statement 2.2. However, when you look at the information contained in the chart this statement could be deemed as being superficial and a low scalar for that behavioural statement would be awarded.

However, if you refer to the chart and say, 'You have the lowest number of files submitted on time compared to the rest of the team. Constables Morley and Butler have 100 per cent and all of the other team members are above the 80 per cent divisional target'. This would also score the behavioural statement but would be awarded a higher scalar.

If this approach were taken to all three charts then a high overall grade for this competency area would be the result. However, do not spend four minutes explaining the charts, there are other issues for you to address.

2.4 Acknowledges role actors' experience/arrests. I have mentioned previously that it is essential that you maintain a balanced view when dealing with Ho. This behavioural statement would be scored when referring to Ho's overall arrest rate (perhaps as a result of responding to role actor response 7) or acknowledging the information in

Sergeant Weller's memorandum referring to the robbery operation or the fact that Ho is well respected in the area.

2.5 Outlines need to balance arrests/investigations. Clearly Ho is under the impression that making arrests is the most important aspect of their work. This is obviously not the case and this fact needs to be outlined to Ho.

Area 3: Problem Solving

This area contains four behavioural statements. Notice that the first two are prefixed by 'Suggests'. The scalar for this area is Clear to Unclear.

3.1 ... attachment to the File Checking Unit. Quite clearly the candidate information suggests that Ho has difficulty with file submission quality and timeliness. What better place to gain an appreciation of these aspects than the File Checking Unit? This suggestion would result in the role actor delivering response 9.

3.2 ... methods to manage files/workload. Suggestions could range from shadowing other team members, mentoring by other team members who have achieved 100 per cent file timeliness or sufficient to proceed or even ensuring that Ho puts aside time to compile files. Whatever you suggest to address the under performance in relation to the files would score this behavioural statement. This suggestion would result in the role actor delivering response 9.

3.3 Offers self as support. You are Ho's line manager and irrespective of their under performance you should offer your assistance. Remember to consider how you would like to be treated if you were in Ho's position.

3.4 Informs role actor will monitor future workload. This behavioural statement could be scored in a supportive way to ensure that Ho is not being inundated with work or as a method of you ensuring file targets are met.

Area 4: Resilience

This area contains the minimum three behavioural statements. Notice that the last two are prefixed by 'Outlines consequences'. The scalar for this area is Clear to Unclear.

4.1 Informs role actor that phone number was incorrect. Ho is unaware of this fact and that it is the reason why the File Checking Unit staff could not contact the witness. It is another indication of Ho's lack of attention to detail.

4.2 ... of poor quality/late submission of files. Remember to explain the consequences. Examples could be losing the case at court or the effect on victims.

4.3 ... of discontinuance of Kennedy case. This refers to the report in the local press and as a consequence how the police may be viewed. The effect on the cricket club itself should also be considered as it has been subject to a number of offences of criminal damage, as should be the issue of how the members would now view the police.

Area 5: Respect for Race and Diversity

As I previously mentioned, this competency area does not contain behavioural statements. You are assessed across the five-minute interaction against two scalars, in this case Constructive to Dismissive and Supportive to Unsupportive.

It is essential to maintain a balanced view when dealing with the exercises. If you focus on the negative aspects such as the under performance in relation to the Kennedy case and file submissions you would miss offering your support to Ho and acknowledging their good work in relation to the number of arrests, the robbery operation and the respect they have in the community. This would affect your overall Respect for Race and Diversity grade.

Candidate instructions

In this exercise you will receive two pages of preparatory information:

- a memorandum from Inspector Tait
- a sickness report

During the activity phase you will meet Constable T Lamber.

CASTLESHIRE POLICE

Memorandum

From:	Inspector Tait, Castleside
To:	Sergeant 'Candidate', Team 5, Castleside
Subject:	Constable T Lamber
Date:	yesterday

I have today been approached by Sergeant Perwaze from the Resourcing Unit who expressed concern regarding one of your team members, Constable Lamber.

The Resourcing Unit has been tasked with providing a number of trained search team officers to assist with a large scale national conference to be held outside the force area in three weeks' time. This is a major event and requires officers from Castleshire to be away from the force area for the one-week duration of the event.

Constable Lamber qualified as a national search team operative three months ago. However, the officer has been on sick leave for the last five weeks due to a muscular injury and is undergoing treatment supervised by the force Occupational Health Department (OHD).

Sergeant Perwaze states that she was contacted by Constable Lamber who asked to be allocated search team duties at this conference. When Sergeant Perwaze pointed out that this was not possible due to Constable Lamber being on sick leave she states that the officer said: "It's alright sarge, I'm sure I can manage the week. If need be I'll go sick again after." I am somewhat surprised at Constable Lamber's attitude.

For your information, Constable Lamber has 14 years' police service, the last five years as a member of team 5. The officer is well regarded by colleagues as being a conscientious officer. However, during the last six months the officer has suffered a number of periods of sickness. The officer is attending OHD on your first day here. I have asked the officer to call and see you after their appointment at the OHD. I have attached a copy of the officer's sickness record.

L Tait

Inspector

SICKNESS RECORD

Constable T Lamber

The following record relates to absence during the last three years.

Date	Days Sick	Reason
2 years ago	1	Migraine
7 months ago	7	Sprained Ankle
5 months ago	3	Stomach upset
4 months ago	2	Sore Throat
3 months ago	3	Stomach upset
2 months ago	2	Migraine
5 weeks ago to present	Ongoing	Muscular injury

Castleshire Police operates a scoring system based on a numerical figure calculated by taking into account the frequency and length of absence.

It is calculated by multiplying the number of periods of absence squared by the total number of days lost. A numerical total of 300 within the previous 12 months is the threshold figure.

Constable Lamber's score is calculated as follows:

7 months ago	$1 \times 1 \times 7 = 7$
5 months ago	$2 \times 2 \times 10 = 40$
4 months ago	$3 \times 3 \times 12 = 108$
3 months ago	$4 \times 4 \times 15 = 240$
2 months ago	$5 \times 5 \times 17 = 425$

The officers' current period of absence is not calculated in this report, as it is currently ongoing. As can be seen from Constable Lamber's sickness record the officer has exceed the threshold figure and therefore is not eligible for consideration for promotion, transfer or lateral development, save in exceptional circumstances.

Candidate information debrief

This exercise uses numerical data in the form of tables to give you experience in dealing with data in this format. How did you cope with the data and the explanation of how the sickness score was calculated? Some candidates can be fazed when confronted with tables containing numerical information or data but practising with these exercises will help you become more familiar with this format.

Did you find you had sufficient time to read through the two pages of information? Both pages contain a lot of information so you need to use your time well. By now you should have realised that you do not have time to rewrite the exercise.

Memorandum from Inspector Tait

It is apparent from the opening two paragraphs of Inspector Tait's memorandum that the exercise refers to Constable Lamber and a forthcoming event occurring outside of the Castleshire Police area where the force has been requested to provide search team trained officers. The event will last for one week.

Lamber qualified as a search team operative three months ago but has been on sick leave for the past five weeks with a muscular injury. Did you consider what the cause of this injury might be? Did you consider it might be work related?

Lamber is presently undergoing treatment for this injury, which is being supervised by the force Occupational Health Department (OHD). Did you consider you might need information regarding the progress of this injury?

The next paragraph should have caused you some concern, it certainly did with Inspector Tait. Lamber has requested to be allowed to accompany the search team to the out-of-force event despite being on sick leave. Lamber has intimated a return to sick leave after the event is concluded. You may want to address this comment when you meet Lamber.

The memorandum then provides you with details of Lamber's police service and the fact that they are well regarded by colleagues as being a conscientious officer. No doubt you will have identified this information as a positive aspect to Lamber's performance. Remember to balance the positive aspects with the negative aspects. Significantly, the memorandum informs you that Lamber has recently had a number of periods of sickness. This information has added another issue to the exercise and suggests that the problem is not just confined to the present period of sickness but is far more reaching. The first question that should have struck you is, why so many periods of sickness?

The final paragraph informs you that Lamber has just attended an appointment at the OHD. You may consider this as unimportant but remember to read all of the candidate information – as you will find out it may be significant.

Sickness record

The sickness record contains detailed information of Lamber's absences over the past three years. The table contains some important information for you to use or clarify during your meeting with Lamber.

- It is apparent that the level of sickness reports has increased over the past seven months. The only report previous to this period was two years ago. Why should this be the case?
- The number of days on sick leave over the periods relating to the last seven months ranges from two days to seven. Is this significant? What is the reason for this?
- The present period of sick leave commenced five weeks ago and is still ongoing. Why is this the case?
- The reasons for the sick leave periods also vary and are for minor ailments. This eliminates the fact that Lamber could be suffering from the same ongoing health problem.

As you can see, the table has produced a number of issues for you to clarify with Lamber.

The remainder of the sickness report then explains the Castleshire sickness policy. I appreciate that at a first glance the system employed looks complex as it contains mathematical calculations. Rest assured there is no need to re do the calculations. The significant figures for you to concentrate on are the threshold figure and Lamber's personal score, as this has a bearing on any future role they are able to perform. Bear in mind this is force policy and something you cannot change.

Role actor instructions

You are Terry/Terri Lamber, a constable with 14 years police service. The past five years you have worked at Castleside as a member of team 5.

You are married and have two children; twin girls aged three years. Until five months ago your wife/husband worked as sales executive for a leading marketing company. It was a well-paid position and provided a comfortable lifestyle for your family, including the employment of a nanny who assisted in the care of your children. The marketing company was taken over by a multi-national company and relocated to America resulting in your wife/husband giving up their position. This has caused some financial hardship, although you are managing to make ends meet, you can no longer afford childcare provision. This has resulted in you taking periods of sickness whilst your wife/husband seeks further employment. You realise that this is wrong however you do not know what else you can do.

You are a conscientious officer who gets on well with colleagues. You are happy with your position as a member of team 5. You intend to start preparing for the promotion examination next year.

You are not aware of the scoring system of absence monitoring. If it is explained to you, willingly accept the situation regarding promotion/development. You have exceeded the threshold score of 300 but were unaware of this.

Your current absence is genuine and is due to a torn muscle in your shoulder sustained in a fall at your home five weeks ago. You will acknowledge that the previous sickness incidents referred to were not genuine but were given to cover your absence whilst looking after your children. Your previous supervisor, Sergeant Weller, was unaware of the reason for you reporting sick on the occasions prior to your present sickness report.

Demeanour: quiet and subdued.

When you enter the room, say:

1. **"Hello Inspector I'm Terry/Terri Lamber I understand you want to see me."**

   If the candidate explains the reason for meeting, say:

2.   **"Yes I know I've been off a while now."**

If the candidate asks what happened at your visit to the OHD, say:

3.   **"They said I should be fully fit in four weeks."**

If the candidate asks you about your request to attend the search team deployment, say:

4.   **"I've had all the training and it would be a good opportunity to make a bit of cash."**

If the candidate asks why you requested search team duty whilst on the sick, say:

5.   **"It won't be a problem, I know I'm okay. I'm about ready to come back anyway."**

If the candidate asks about your current illness, say:

6.   **"I'm feeling okay, things are much better now."**

If the candidate asks you about or raises the issue of your sickness record/score, say:

7.   **"It's been really difficult with having to look after the twins. I thought it would only have been a few days."**

If the candidate asks about the situation at home, say:

8.   **"Since my wife/husband was made redundant it's been difficult to cope. The nanny has had to go."**

If the candidate asks for more information about the situation at home, say:

9.   **"We just about manage to make ends meet. As you can imagine the loss of the other income has hit us hard."**

If the candidate outlines welfare support/options to assist with childcare, say:

10. **"I didn't realise the job could help. That would be a help to us."**

If the candidate asks if you made the comment to Sergeant Perwaze, say:

11. **"Yes but I'm sure I'll be fine and I want to have the opportunity to use the Search Team training."**

If the candidate outlines abuse of the sickness policy, say:

12. "I understand, I just didn't know what to do."

If the candidate states that you must comply with sickness policy in future, say:

13. "I appreciate that. It won't happen again."

If the candidate mentions the implications of exceeding the sickness threshold, say:

14. "I'm disappointed but I understand. I will work hard to improve it."

Role actor instructions debrief

The Lamber role actor has the answer to all of your queries. However, when interacting with the role actor do not spend the greater proportion of your time asking the role actor a lot of questions.

The Lamber exercise is not a gender specific exercise. Lamber is an experienced constable with 14 years' police service. The officer has been a member of team 5 at Castleside for the past five years.

The role actor instructions outline domestic issues that have seriously affected the Lamber household. As a candidate this is the information you require and will provide you with the reason as to why Lamber has been taking periods of sick leave.

Lamber is a conscientious officer who is well regarded by their peers. This information, together with Lamber's domestic circumstances, would appear to indicate that Lamber has found themselves in a position where they would prefer not to be. You may consider that Lamber requires support rather than being taken to task over their sickness record.

As you can see from the role actor instructions, Lamber's present period of sickness is genuine following a fall at home five weeks before. You will also notice that Lamber is not a confrontational role actor, in fact quite the contrary.

Role actor response 1 merely confirms the role actor's name and the fact they have been asked to see you. This is a standard role actor opening line. Always allow the role actor to deliver their opening line as they enter the assessment centre room.

Role actor response 2 strikes a conciliatory tone and indicates that perhaps Lamber was expecting a meeting regarding their current period of sickness.

Role actor response 3 provides you with the information you may have identified as requiring when you read about the latest OHD appointment in Inspector Tait's memorandum. You will notice in Inspector Tait's memorandum that the out-of-force event takes place in three weeks' time. This role actor response indicates that Lamber will be fully fit in four weeks, obviously after the event has taken place. This is an example of how you can use information from one source, in this case the role actor, to support or address information in another, the candidate information. This response from Lamber should now inform your decision regarding their attendance at the event.

Role actor response 4 outlines Lamber's reason for wanting to attend the event. How would you respond to this information? Perhaps you would like to seek clarification, in which case role actor response 5 would provide you with the information. However, Lamber's views do not correlate with the opinion of the OHD. You need to point this out to Lamber.

Role actor response 6 provides you with the information you require to clarify the position regarding the current period of sickness.

Role actor response 7 is the key to the exercise. What was your initial reaction when you read the response? How would you respond to this information? You would not have been wrong to identify that Lamber has breached the Code of Conduct. However, your first reaction should have been to seek further information regarding Lamber's domestic situation. That would result in role actor responses 8 and 9. Once you have responded, you can then offer your support or suggestions to assist Lamber. This would then result in role actor response 10. In a few sentences I have more or less described how an interaction with a role actor could take place. Your responses to the role actor should follow a natural progression responding to the information they provide. However, do not forget to continue to refer to the candidate information.

There are still other issues in the exercise to address, for example the comment to Sergeant Perwaze in relation to returning to sick leave once the event is over. Role actor response 11 suggests that Lamber only wants to go to the event in order to maintain his search team skills. You may feel it necessary that the comment made to Sergeant Perwaze requires addressing. It certainly does not reflect well on Lamber.

By addressing the issues outlined in the prompts for role actor responses 12, 13 and 14 you are displaying your potential to perform in the Sergeant rank. Each one of the prompts outlines you pointing out the implications of Lamber's actions. You have to address a role actor's under performance at some point during your five-minute interaction. It does not matter where this occurs during the interaction.

Assessment checklist

Competency Area	Scalar	Grade
Area 1: Effective Communication **Asks role actor:** 1.1 reason for sickness 1.2 result of latest OHD appointment 1.3 why requesting search team duties 1.4 if sought any assistance for childcare problem 1.5 if previous supervision aware of true reasons for absence	Thorough – Superficial 1 2 3 4 5	A B C D
Area 2: Effective Communication **Explains:** 2.1 sickness policy re the 'scoring index' 2.2 implications re promotion, lateral development 2.3 could be subject to discipline procedures 2.4 effect on team (increased workload etc) 2.5 must contact self/other supervisor with any further sickness 2.6 reporting sick when not ill will stop	Thorough – Superficial 1 2 3 4 5	A B C D
Area 3: Planning and Organising **Outlines:** 3.1 consideration to flexible working 3.2 implications of returning when not fit/recovered 3.3 not be allowed to accompany search team	Purposeful – Vague 1 2 3 4 5	A B C D
Area 4: Maximising Potential **Outlines:** 4.1 availability of welfare support 4.2 will monitor future sickness reports 4.3 well regarded/conscientious officer 4.4 has exceeded sickness threshold score	Clear – Unclear 1 2 3 4 5	A B C D
Area 5: Respect for Race and Diversity	Objective – Biased 1 2 3 4 5 Sensitive – Insensitive 1 2 3 4 5	A B C D

Assessment checklist debrief

As you can see the Lamber exercise contains the maximum five competency areas; Problem Solving, Effective Communication, Planning and Organising, Maximising Potential and Respect for Race and Diversity.

The exercise also contains the maximum 18 behavioural statements (statements a candidate should say). Remember there will be no more than six and no less than three behavioural statements in a competency area. Respect for Race and Diversity does not contain behavioural statements.

We will now take each competency area and behavioural statement in turn. Have your candidate information and role actor notes to hand to see which behavioural statements you would have scored.

Area 1: Problem Solving
This area contains five behavioural statements. Notice that all are prefixed by 'Asks role actor'. The scalar (how well a candidate scores the behavioural statements) for this area is Thorough to Superficial.

1.1 ... reason for sickness. As I mentioned in the role actor instructions debrief, this is the key to exercise. Receiving this information, in the form of role actor response 7, would enable you to address the issue that underpins the exercise. However, as you will see, failure to ask this question would not preclude you from scoring behavioural statements not connected with Lamber's domestic circumstances.

1.2 ... result of latest OHD appointment. You do not know the result. As Inspector Tait outlines in their memorandum, Lamber has only attended their latest appointment that day. Perhaps the OHD deemed Lamber fit for duty. The information you are seeking is contained in role actor response 3.

1.3 ... why requesting search team duties. Having identified that Lamber is currently on sick leave you must have been curious as to why they are requesting search team duties. Role actor response 4 would provide you with the information.

1.4 ... if sought any assistance for childcare problem. Perhaps Lamber has already sought assistance with the domestic circumstances. This would then reduce the options you could offer. Lamber has not sought assistance so this should lead you on to offering suggestions to assist.

1.5 ... if previous supervision aware of true reasons for absence. You need to know this. If Sergeant Weller was aware, then what assistance or action was taken? The fact that Sergeant Weller was unaware is contained in the role actor Instructions.

Area 2: Effective Communication
This area contains the maximum six behavioural statements. Notice that all are prefixed by 'Explains'. The scalar for this area is Thorough to Superficial.

2.1 ... sickness policy re the 'scoring index'. This behavioural statement refers to the information contained in the sickness report (paragraph 2 after table). The role actor instructions outline that Lamber is not aware of the scoring system.

2.2 ... implications re promotion, lateral development. This information is also contained in the sickness report (last paragraph). The implications would also refer to the search team duties.

2.3 ... could be subject to discipline procedures. As I mentioned in the role actor instructions debrief, once you had established the reason for the sickness reports (role actor response 7), your immediate reaction may have been to consider a breach of the Code of Conduct. The fact that Lamber has put themselves in jeopardy should be outlined.

2.4 ... effect on team (increased workload etc). This is an organisational consequence of Lamber reporting sick when not ill.

2.5 ... must contact self/other supervisor with any further sickness. This behavioural statement is about you as the team supervisor imposing conditions on any future sickness reports.

2.6 ... reporting sick when not ill will stop. Once the reason for the sickness reports has been established you should point this out immediately, regardless of Lamber's domestic circumstances. However, ensure that you do this within the bounds of Respect for Race and Diversity.

Area 3: Planning and Organising

This area contains the minimum three behavioural statements. Notice that all are prefixed by 'Outlines'. The scalar for this area is Purposeful to Vague.

3.1 ... consideration to flexible working. Flexible working could be an option to suggest to Lamber to assist with their domestic circumstances.

3.2 ... implications of returning when not fit/recovered. This behavioural statement could be a response to role actor responses 4 or 5. For example, you could outline that Lamber risks suffering further injury or further aggravating the torn shoulder injury which would result in incurring more sick leave.

3.3 ... not be allowed to accompany search team. You must make this decision in the light of the information given by the OHD that Lamber will not be fully fit for a further four weeks (role actor response 3). You have no option as the event is being held in three weeks' time. Role actor response 14 would be the result of outlining this decision.

Area 4: Maximising Potential

This area contains four behavioural statements. Notice that all are prefixed by 'Outlines'. The scalar for this area is Clear to Unclear.

4.1 ... availability of welfare support. The offer of assistance to Lamber could include the use of force resources such as welfare support.

4.2 ... will monitor future sickness reports. This behavioural statement is similar to those at 2.5 and 2.6. It is about you taking on the role of the team supervisor to ensure there is not a repeat of false sickness reports.

4.3 ... well regarded/conscientious officer. I have mentioned previously that you must not only focus on the negative aspects of a person's performance. Although in this exercise it may be tempting to focus on the false sickness reports, it is still essential that you maintain a balanced view. The information regarding Lamber's positive past performance is contained in Inspector Tait's memorandum.

4.4 ... has exceeded sickness threshold score. This information could be gleaned from the sickness report. The threshold is 300 and, even without taking the present sickness period into account, Lamber has a 'score' of 425. You could outline this to Lamber then go onto explain that they will not be allowed to accompany the search team (behavioural statement 3.3). Remember, it does not matter at which point you score a behavioural statement during your five-minute interaction. If you say it, you score it.

Area 5: Respect for Race and Diversity

As I previously mentioned this competency area does not contain behavioural statements. You are assessed across the five-minute interaction against two scalars, in this case Objective to Biased and Sensitive to Insensitive.

It is possible that candidates could just focus on the false sickness reports issue and fail to recognise or elicit the reason why Lamber has falsely been reporting sick. However, once the reason has been obtained you should be sensitive to Lamber's domestic circumstances.

Candidate instructions

In this exercise you will receive two pages of preparatory information:

- a memorandum from Sergeant Weller
- a copy of an email from Detective Sergeant Craddock

During the activity phase you will meet Constable C Morley.

CASTLESHIRE POLICE

Memorandum

From:	Sergeant Weller
To:	Sergeant 'Candidate', team 5, Castleside
Subject:	Constable Morley
Date:	yesterday

I have attached a copy of an e-mail from Detective Sergeant Craddock, concerning a performance issue with Constable Morley. I have spoken with Acting Sergeant Avis as she was covering for me on the day concerned and she confirms that Constable Morley was instructed to protect the scene following an alleged rape. However, she has no knowledge of Constable Morley attending an attack alarm and does not recall any radio transmissions that the officer was attending the alarm.

Acting Sergeant Avis also made me aware of an incident last week where Constable Morley was on patrol with Special Constable Iles. They came across some insecure premises with a ladder leading up to an open first floor window. Before the key holder or back up arrived, Constable Morley climbed the ladder and checked the premises. It later transpired the owner had been carrying out some repairs and had forgotten about the ladder.

Constable Morley has two and a half years service and has let themselves down with these incidents, which are out of character. Under my supervision, I have always found the officer to be reliable and able to be trusted to work with minimum supervision. Additionally, the quality of their work in general is an example to the others on the team.

I have been unable to speak with Constable Morley as the officer has been on leave for two days, so I have arranged for the officer to meet with you on your first day.

J Weller

Sergeant

Email Printout	

From:	Detective Sergeant Craddock, Castleside CID
To:	Sergeant Weller, team 5
Date:	yesterday
Subject:	Constable Morley – performance issue
Security:	RESTRICTED

I am really disappointed to bring this to your attention but I feel your team's reputation is being let down by Constable Morley.

Last Thursday morning, following an allegation of rape, Peter Ian Meadows was arrested at his home address of Flat 3, Castle Towers, Castleside. Constable Morley was directed to guard the premises until the Crime Scene Investigator attended. However, when the investigator arrived, they found the cleaner about to enter the flat with their own key and there was no sign of Constable Morley.

Constable Morley appeared some five minutes later having apparently self-deployed to an attack alarm activation at a nearby building society.

Fortunately, the Crime Scene Investigator managed to send the cleaner away. However, I have to question how Constable Morley completed their probation. I think it best you speak to them as this issue has already tested my patience to the limit.

Jenny Craddock

Detective Sergeant
Castleside CID

Candidate information debrief

This exercise contains a little less candidate information than previous exercises. Nevertheless, there are still a number of issues for you to address in your meeting with Morley. The subject of health and safety is any everyday issue in the workplace and certainly an issue addressed on a daily basis by sergeants. Similarly, crime scene preservation is a subject of the utmost importance to the service. However, in a Part II exercise, no one issue or subject contained in an exercise carries any more weight than another.

Memorandum from Sergeant Weller

The opening paragraph indicates that the information regarding Constable Morley has originated from Detective Sergeant Craddock. The e-mail refers to a performance issue with Constable Morley. At this stage there is no indication as to what this may be, so keep an open mind. The paragraph then continues by suggesting that the performance may be in relation to Constable Morley's actions at the scene of an alleged rape. So at this point there is still no indication as to what the issue(s) may be. The information referring to Constable Morley attending an attack alarm could be an indication as to what has occurred. However, perhaps there was a reason Constable Morley attended the attack alarm and may have a connection with the alleged rape scene?

The memorandum then continues by outlining an incident the previous week involving Constable Morley and Special Constables Iles at the scene of insecure premises.

What is your impression of Morley in the light of these two incidents? Do you consider they may have acted irresponsibly? Bear in mind that you do not as yet have the full facts relating to either incident.

The next paragraph provides you with information regarding Morley. The officer only has two and a half years service and appears to have acted out of character. Sergeant Weller has always found the officer to be reliable and able to work with the minimum of supervision. In fact the quality of Morley's work is of a good standard. So what could be the reason for this type of behaviour at the two incidents outlined?

Email from Detective Sergeant Craddock

The email commences by outlining that Detective Sergeant Craddock feels that team 5's reputation has been tarnished by Morley's actions.

This should be a concern to you as the team sergeant.

This email provides you with further information in relation to Morley's actions at the alleged rape scene. You should have made notes in relation to the consequences, not only to Morley personally, but also to the potential of the alleged rape scene being compromised.

The email concludes with Detective Sergeant Craddock questioning Morley's competence and the information that she is clearly unimpressed by Morley's performance.

This is a straightforward exercise - it is an everyday issue that sergeants are required to address. Remember, the exercises you will undertake at your actual assessment centre are based on common issues encountered by a sergeant.

Role actor instructions

You are Carl/Carla Morley. You are single and have two and a half years' service, which has all been at Castleside. You have decided that you would like to specialise on one of the divisional crime teams and think that you need to raise your profile by increasing your arrest rate.

Last Tuesday, at 20.00 hours you were out on patrol with Special Constable Iles when you came across a ladder leading up to an open first floor window at the rear of Joe's Bakery in Castle Street. Thinking this could lead to a good arrest, you decided to climb the ladder and check the premises yourself before the key holder or back up arrived. It later transpired the owner had been carrying out some repairs and had forgotten about the ladder.

On Thursday morning, you were directed by Acting Sergeant Avis to protect the scene of an alleged rape at Flat 3, Castle Towers, Castleside, having been left with the keys to the premises. At 08.45 hours, you were waiting outside in the communal hallway when you monitored a call of an attack alarm at the Castleshire Building Society. As the premises were only around the corner in the High Street, you decided to self-deploy but did not inform the communication centre. The alarm was a false activation and when you returned to the flat, the Crime Scene Investigator was waiting outside the premises with the cleaner who had her own set of keys.

You are well thought of by Sergeant Weller and have prided yourself on the quality of your paperwork. The only health and safety training you have received was the input during your initial training.

Demeanour: confident

When you enter the room, say:

1. **"Hello Sergeant I'm Carl/Carla Morley. Sergeant Weller left me a note to come and see you."**

    If the candidate asks for details about the ladder incident, say:

2. **"We were in town during the early evening when we came across the insecure premises."**

    If the candidate asks why you entered the premises before waiting for back up or keyholder, say:

3. **"I was just thinking about the arrest."**

If the candidate points out the health and safety issues, say:

4.   "I hadn't considered that. I wasn't on my own and Special Constable Iles held the ladder."

If the candidate states that you should have waited for the key holder/back-up, say:

5.   "I thought Special Constable Iles and I could handle the situation."

If the candidate points out the need to carry out dynamic risk assessments, say:

6.   "I take your point. I'll make sure I do that in future."

If the candidate asks for details about the alleged rape scene premises you were detailed to protect, say:

7.   "The flat was secured. I had the owner's set of keys as he was in custody at the station."

If the candidate asks why you left the scene to attend the alarm activation, say:

8.   "I thought it was more of a priority and I was only around the corner."

If the candidate asks why you did not inform your supervisor/communication centre that you were attending, say:

9.   "I didn't see the point as they were sending a car anyway."

If the candidate outlines the consequences of your actions at the scene of the alleged rape, say:

10.   "I can see what you are saying, but I didn't think anyone else would have a set of keys to the flat."

If the candidate asks why these events have occurred/are out of character, say:

11.   "I want to try and increase my arrest rate. I want to raise my profile as I'd like to specialise at some point."

If the candidate outlines the positive comments from Sergeant Weller, say:

12.   "Thanks sergeant. I really enjoy the job and we've got a good team."

If the candidate makes suggestions for your future development, say:

13.   "If you think that will help. I'm willing to try anything."

Role actor instructions debrief

As you can see the Morley exercise is not gender specific. What is important is the fact that Morley is a relatively inexperienced police officer with only two and a half years' service. Despite this inexperience, Morley has decided that they would like to specialise on one of the divisional crime teams. Consequently, they feel that in order to do this they should increase their profile by increasing their arrest rate.

There are a couple of issues for you as the team sergeant to consider here. Is Morley, with so little experience, ready for a specialist post? If so, how can you support the officer? Why does Morley feel that the only way of raising their profile is to increase their arrest rate?

The role actor instructions contain information about the incidents outlined in the candidate information.

The final paragraph outlines the fact that Morley is well thought of by Sergeant Weller and Morley prides themselves on the high standard of their paperwork. Both positive traits that were mentioned in Sergeant Weller's memorandum. Finally, and perhaps significantly in the light of the insecure premises incident, Morley received health and safety training during their initial training.

As you will have noticed when you read through the role actor lines Morley is not a confrontational role actor.

Role actor response 1 is the standard opening line and confirms the role actor's identity. This is done for the candidate's benefit as a way of confirming whom they are meeting. It can happen that a candidate becomes confused if an exercise contains three or four names. If you find you have misread the information and thought you were meeting someone different to the role actor, the best advice I can offer is to still work your way through your candidate information notes. Always bear in mind that the name of the exercise is always the name of the role actor.

Role actor response 2 provides you with details about the insecure premises. I'm sure you identified that you want more details about this incident.

Role actor response 3 requires a response from you in respect of health and safety. At this point, you may also want to enquire as to why Morley finds it so important to focus on the arrests.

Role actor response 4 is the response you would receive should you point out to Morley the health and safety issues. You can then enquire as to what health and safety training Morley has received.

Role actor response 5 could lead you into suggesting that in future Morley carries out a risk assessment at the scene of an incident and why this is necessary. That suggestion would result in role actor response 6.

It is clear from Detective Sergeant Craddock's e-mail that Morley has compromised the alleged rape scene by leaving it to attend the attack alarm. As Morley's supervisor you need further details of this incident, and in particular the reason why Morley left the scene. The relevant question would result in the delivery of either role actor response 7 or 8.

Role actor response 9 suggests that you need to reinforce the health and safety aspects of Morley's actions. However, bear in mind that you can address the issues in any order you wish during your five-minute interaction with Morley. Asking the question outlined in the prompt for role actor response 9 could be your first question or your last, it does not matter. Similarly the role actor is not expected to deliver their responses in the order printed on their role actor instructions.

Role actor response 10 is Morley offering an explanation of their actions at the alleged rape scene.

Role actor response 11 is perhaps the information you are seeking that will lead you to addressing a number of issues, such as health and safety, or perhaps pointing out to Morley that arrests are not the most important part of police work. This response should also lead you into asking what Morley's career aspirations are.

Role actor response 12 could lead you into linking your two sources of information: the candidate information and the role actor. In the candidate information Detective Sergeant Craddock points out in her email that the reputation of team 5 'is being let down by Constable Morley'. In role actor response 12, Morley states 'and we've got a good team'. The reputation of the team, your team, in the division could be affected by Morley's actions. Perhaps this should be addressed with Detective Sergeant Craddock.

Role actor response 13 shows that Morley is willing to try anything in their development. It is always worth including a role actor in the decision making process or asking for their opinion on a proposed course of action.

Assessment checklist

Competency Area	Scalar	Grade

Area 1: Effective Communication
Asks role actor for details about:

Thorough – Superficial
1 2 3 4 5   A B C D

1.1 insecure premises incident
1.2 the insecure premises
1.3 protecting scene of crime
1.4 health and safety training received
1.5 career aspirations

Area 2: Maximising Potential
Outlines potential consequences:

Thorough – Superficial
1 2 3 4 5   A B C D

2.1 of actions at insecure premises (eg. health and safety/risk)
2.2 of leaving scene of rape (eg. loss of evidence)
2.3 to role actor of actions at incidents (eg. discipline)
2.4 Acknowledges role actor's previous performance
2.5 Suggests attending health and safety training
2.6 Offers self as support with role actor's development

Area 3: Planning and Organising
Outlines:

Thorough – Superficial
1 2 3 4 5   A B C D

3.1 duty of care to Special Constable Iles
3.2 need to dynamic risk assess
3.3 impression given to CID/DS Craddock
3.4 Suggests meeting with DS Craddock
3.5 Explains must not self deploy
3.6 Explains must keep supervisor/comm centre updated

Area 4: Respect for Race and Diversity

Constructive – Dismissive
1 2 3 4 5
Supportive - Unsupportive
1 2 3 4 5

Assessment checklist debrief

The Morley exercise contains four competency areas; Effective Communication, Maximising Potential, Resilience and Respect for Race and Diversity.

The exercise also contains 17 behavioural statements (statements a candidate should say).

We will now take each competency area and behavioural statement in turn. Have your candidate information and role actor notes to hand to see which behavioural statements you would have scored.

Area 1: Effective Communication

This area contains five behavioural statements. Notice that all are prefixed by 'Asks role actor for details about'. The scalar (how well a candidate scores the behavioural statements) for this area is Thorough to Superficial.

1.1 ... insecure premises incident. You are new to the team and need to gather as much information as you can concerning the incidents in which Morley has been involved. This question would result in the delivery of role actor response 2.

1.2 ... the insecure premises. The nature of the premises is not identified in the candidate information. You could ask the question at behavioural statement 1.1 then follow it up by clarifying the nature of the premises or vice versa. Either way you would score the behavioural statements.

1.3 ... protecting scene of crime. This question would result in the delivery of role actor response 7. This question is once again about you trying to build up a picture about the incidents. Look upon it as evidence gathering and piecing together information from different sources.

1.4 ... health and safety training received. You need to clarify Morley's level of awareness in respect of health and safety. Obviously they have only received training fairly recently during their initial training.

1.5 ... career aspirations. This question could be following on from role actor response 11, clarifying what Morley wants to specialise in.

Area 2: Maximising Potential

This area contains the maximum six behavioural statements. Notice that the first three are prefixed by 'Outlines potential consequences' The scalar for this area is Thorough to Superficial.

2.1 ... of actions at insecure premises. The consequences could be outlined following the delivery of role actor response 3, 4 or 5. You may have already identified the consequences as you read through the candidate information. No doubt you will have considered the health and safety risks as well as the fact that Morley and Special Constable Iles were put at risk. There is also the impression given to Special Constable Iles that they may consider such actions acceptable.

2.2 ... of leaving scene of rape. I have already alluded to these consequences such as the scene being compromised or loss of evidence.

2.3 ... to role actor of actions at incidents. It is certainly worth mentioning the possible personal consequences to Morley of the actions undertaken at both incidents. This could be regarding discipline, their reputation being affected, or the effect on any future post applications. You must bear in mind that Morley wants to specialise on a divisional crime team and that the e-mail of complaint was received from a Detective Sergeant.

2.4 Acknowledges role actor's previous performance. Despite Morley's actions at the scene, the candidate information does contain positive aspects of their performance. Pointing out the positive aspects would result in the delivery of role actor response 12.

2.5 Suggests attending health and safety training. You may feel this necessary, as although Morley received Health and Safety training during the initial training, a refresher may be required.

2.6 Offers self as support with role actor's development. Morley is an inexperienced officer and clearly requires support and guidance if they are to progress in the organisation. They are your responsibility so offer your support.

Area 3: Resilience

This area contains the maximum six behavioural statements. Notice that the first three are prefixed by 'Outlines'. The scalar for this area is

Thorough to Superficial.

3.1 ... duty of care to Special Constable Iles. This behavioural statement could follow on from behavioural statement 2.1.

3.2 ... need to dynamic risk assess. This behavioural statement is about you, as the team supervisor, outlining to Morley what is expected in the future. You could then go onto outline the consequences of not risk assessing. Addressing the need to risk assess would result in the delivery of role actor response 6.

3.3 ... impression given to CID/DS Craddock. This is clearly outlined in Detective Sergeant Craddock's email. It could be the impression of team 5 or Morley.

3.4 Suggests meeting with DS Craddock. This would help restore relations with Detective Sergeant Craddock who states in her email that 'this issue has already tested my patience to the limit'.

3.5 Explains must not self deploy. This behavioural statement is also about you taking on the role of team 5 supervisor and clearly outlining future expectations.

3.6 Explains must keep supervisor/comm. centre updated. This is similar to behavioural statement 3.5 and would result in the delivery of role actor response 9. You would then have to respond to Morley's reasoning. Again this may provide you with an opportunity to introduce health and safety or risk assessment.

Area 4: Respect for Race and Diversity

As I have previously mentioned this competency area does not contain behavioural statements. You are assessed across the five-minute interaction against two scalars, in this case Constructive to Dismissive and Supportive to Unsupportive.

It is essential to maintain a balanced view when dealing with the exercises. If you focus on the negative aspects such as under performance, you would miss offering your support to Morley, which would affect your Respect for Race and Diversity grade.

You should have an appreciation as to why it is essential that you take on the role of a sergeant when dealing with these exercises. There are a number of behavioural statements contained in this exercise that you would not score had you not done this. You do need to address a person's under performance, that is part of the role of a team supervisor, but at the same time you need to offer your support and assistance when required.

Candidate instructions

In this exercise you will receive three pages of preparatory information:

- a memorandum from Inspector Tait
- a copy of an article from the Castleside Chronicle
- analysis on violent crime in Castleside

During the activity phase you will meet L Reed.

RESTRICTED

CASTLESHIRE
POLICE

CASTLESHIRE POLICE

Memorandum

From:	Inspector Tait, Castleside
To:	Sergeant 'Candidate', Team 5, Castleside
Subject:	Henry Street Campaign
Date:	yesterday

I have just received a message that L Reed will be calling into the police station and wants to discuss what the police are doing about the rise in violent crime and the extended opening hours for the town centre pubs. I will not be available and would like you to meet L Reed and address the issues raised.

L Reed is the leader of the newly formed Henry Street Campaign and I have enclosed a copy of a recent press article about the campaign. For your information, Henry Street is located in the town centre area.

Your predecessor, Sergeant Weller, was tasked with putting together an initiative to address the rise in violent crime in the town centre area. I have attached a copy of the latest analysis results that you may find of assistance.

I am attending a conference over the next two days so I have arranged for L Reed to meet you.

L Tait

Inspector Tait

Castleside Chronicle

BOOZE BUSTERS
Residents unite to tackle 24-hour drinking threat

By Simon Howes,
Crime Reporter

WORRIED residents have launched a campaign to claim back their town amid fears that 24-hour drinking will send Castleside into a spiral of decline and lead to an increase in violent crime.

The Henry Street Campaign has been set up to fight an influx of applications from the town's pubs to serve alcohol for even longer hours. Campaigners fear this will have a detrimental effect on the town's character, resulting in noise pollution in the early hours, increased night-time traffic and an increase in vandalism and anti-social behaviour.

One Henry Street resident said: 'Our life is a complete misery already, if you go out in the morning you've got vomit on the pavements and used condoms in the street. We want our pubs back from the yobs who come in and take over.'

One old lady said: 'The noise coming from the pubs is intolerable. My grandchildren often ask when it's going to stop because they can't sleep. My family do not like me going out at night even if it's only to my daughter's house 500 metres away.'

The campaign leader L Reed said: 'Castleside is a bit unique in that the pubs in the town centre are very close together. People start in one pub and then move onto the next causing mayhem and destruction as they go.

'I do not think it is fair that the majority of people in Castleside cannot use or stroll around their town on an evening for fear of drunks and the awful behaviour it produces. Why has it been allowed to get like this in the first place? I bet no other area of the town suffers like we do.

'Violent crime is escalating and the police seem to have little control. These licensing changes are just going to make the problem worse.'

Violent Crime Analysis, CASTLESIDE
Summary of previous months crime

Locality	Total Crime	Alcohol Related	Domestic Related	Notes
Abbeywell	21	9	4	2 x Local authority care home 3 x Granger St 2 x Valley Brook St Majority evening time
Aston Estate	15	4	3	Windermere Ave/Ambleside Close, hot spots. 9 at weekend. Mostly early evening
Bankside	33	0	4	8 x Castleside Hospital 4 x Castleside Leisure Centre 5 x Schools
Weston	11	4	1	Early evening 8 occurring Thurs – Sun.
Town Centre	36	20	3	Main hotspots – Duke St/ Henry St/ Mill St/ Sunderland St 6 in pubs Mostly late evening and early morning at weekends

1. Very high proportion of offenders are known to the victim – as many as 110 of the 116 noted crimes.

2. High number of offences at premises such as hospitals, care homes, leisure centre, pubs and schools.

Candidate information debrief

This is first exercise of the seven where you have had to deal with a non-police role actor.

At the assessment centre all candidates do not deal with the exercises in the same order. Consequently your first two exercises could be one police and one non-police exercise, or two of the same category. It depends on which room number you have been allocated on the assessment centre corridor. Remember, you remain in the same room throughout the assessment process.

I have mentioned previously that no one exercise carries any more weight than another, or is looked upon as being more important than another. All exercises should be treated the same in terms of your preparation, the method you use when dealing with the role actor and the way you address the issues contained in the exercise.

How did you find the candidate information in this exercise? There is a lot to work through and this exercise gives you experience of working with a newspaper article and statistics. Did you find the statistics complex or relatively easy to understand?

Memorandum from Inspector Tait

Only a short memorandum to read and one that sets the scene and provides you with background to the Henry Street Campaign.

This exercise is focussed on the everyday problem of violent crime or the public's perception of violent crime.

Reed is the leader of the newly formed Henry Street Campaign, which has been formed to express local residents' concerns about violent crime in their area.

In the first paragraph of the memorandum, Inspector Tait asks you to meet with Reed to address the issues raised. Notice that it does not state that you should resolve the issues raised. You are not expected to resolve issues in five-minutes.

The third paragraph of the memorandum holds an important piece of information for you. It outlines that Sergeant Weller was tasked with putting together an initiative to address the rise in violent crime. Did you identify this piece of information? It is important as it suggests that something has already been done on the part of the police to address the problem.

Castleside Chronicle article

This article reinforces the belief or perception of the residents that violent crime is spiralling out of control. This is shown, for example, by the comments from the elderly resident who is afraid to leave her home just to walk the 500 metres to her daughter's home. There are a number of issues contained in this article that you would need to address. However, we will look at these and the article in more depth when we debrief the assessment checklist.

Violent Crime analysis

This document does contain a lot of information and at first glance can seem quite complex, but it is clearly divided into the relevant categories and areas within Castleside. Obviously the area of your focus is the Town Centre.

When confronted with a document of this nature do not become overawed by its layout or content. The exercises are not designed in anyway to try and confuse you or make it a test of mathematics. The key point of this document is the comparison of the different localities in relation to the town centre. Using the statistics and information contained in the document will help you to address Reed's perception of the town centre area. I shall review this document in conjunction with the assessment checklist debrief.

Role actor instructions

You are Linda/Len Reed. You are married and have lived in Henry Street, located close to the town centre area of Castleside, all your life. Henry Street is a largely residential street with a number of small shops. You are very proud of your town, and although you have to travel a lot with your work in sales, you have chosen to remain in Castleside because of all the friends and acquaintances you have locally. You have not previously been involved in any local campaigns or action groups.

Over recent years you have seen a gradual change in the town centre. You have noticed more litter and debris from the previous night's activities on the pavements in the morning, particularly at weekends. Whilst you are not affected by the noise from the pubs yourself, you have heard others are. You are aware of many complaints from fellow residents about the Wilbraham Arms located in Henry Street, which has live bands playing late into the evenings. The final straw has come with the government relaxation in licensing legislation. You are fearful that there will be more noise and violence in the town. You have read in the local press that there has been an increase in violent crime.

Henry Street is one of the main roads off the town centre used as a route between many of the pubs. You have chosen to call the group the Henry Street Campaign because it is the street where you live and it is mostly neighbours that you have spoken to about the issues. You think you will have support from about 30 other residents, but have little formally set up. It was your idea to start the campaign; there have been no meetings and none are planned. Your intention is to get press coverage of the issues, raise awareness of residents' concerns through a petition and speaking to the police and council. If this does not work you plan to confront the people causing the nuisance yourselves.

Demeanour: frustrated and angry

When you enter the room, say:

1.   **"Hello Sergeant I'm Linda/Len Reed. I was told I would be meeting the Inspector."**

    If the candidate asks why you wanted the meeting, say:

2.   **"I want to know what the police are going to do about the nightmare that town centre residents have to live through every weekend."**

If the candidate asks for details of incidents in the town centre/Henry Street, say:

3. **"We are fed up with the noise from pubs, fighting in the streets and the mess left on the pavements outside our homes."**

If the candidate asks where the problems are happening, say:

4. **"All over the town centre, it's just not pleasant to go out."**

If the candidate asks why you think the police are not doing anything, say:

5. **"Well the problem seems to be gradually getting worse, and there have been reports in the local press of an increase in violent crime."**

If the candidate asks for details of your campaign, say:

6. **"I'm not sure exactly. We'll probably start with a petition and if that doesn't work we'll confront these yobs ourselves."**

If the candidate asks specifically about problems with licensed premises, say:

7. **"The Wilbraham Arms causes most of the late night noise with music and then shouting as people leave."**

If the candidate says that violent crime is not all alcohol related or that there are other areas where violence is occurring, say:

8. **"You should try living in the town centre, life at weekends when the yobs arrive is unbearable."**

If the candidate suggests how the wider issue of violent crime will be addressed, say:

9. **"That's all well and good, but I'm only interested in the town centre."**

If the candidate suggests working together/putting out a joint press release, say:

10. **"I'll think about it but I want to see some results from police action first."**

If the candidate outlines options to address problems in the town centre/ with licensed premises, say:

11. **"You're the police officer. If you think that will help."**

Role actor instructions debrief

Do you think the exercise has changed now that you have read the role actor instructions? How would deal with Reed? Were you frustrated by some of the role actor responses or find them confrontational?

Once again the exercise is not gender specific. Reed has lived in the area for a number of years, residing in Henry Street, and has no connections with the local council or other campaigning or political groups.

Unfortunately, in recent years Reed has seen an increase in disorder and general anti-social behaviour in their area. Reed only feels this will get worse as the licensing legislation is relaxed.

Henry Street is situated off one of the main town centre roads and consequently is used as a route between many of the pubs. There is a lot of support for the Henry Street Campaign especially with local residents who are also fearful of a rise in violent crime. This is an important point for you and one you will have to address during your meeting with Reed. Also significant is the fact that residents plan to confront troublemakers.

As you can see, Reed's demeanour is frustrated and angry, the first exercise in the book of this nature. You will not know the role actor's demeanour until they enter your room but do not let the fact that they are confrontational have an affect on how you deal with an exercise. The issues contained in the candidate information have not changed and will still need to be addressed. Do not, however, be sucked in by a role actor's demeanour. The last thing you want to happen is to enter into an argument or protracted discussion about one issue contained in the exercise or a comment made by the role actor.

The previous exercises have all contained straightforward opening role actor responses. The Reed exercise is different in that it suggests that Reed was expecting to meet the Inspector. You will be able to address this by using the information in Inspector Tait's memorandum that they are attending a conference.

Inspector Tait's memorandum does not actually outline the reason why Reed wants to speak to you. It only states that it is in relation to violent crime but does not go into specific detail. You can see from role actor response 2 that Reed is very angry and concerned at what they perceive to be a lack of police action.

Reed lives in the area while you are new to the area. They have a far clearer picture of what is happening in the area. Role actor response 3 provides you with these details.

Role actor response 4 tends to suggest that the problem is more widespread than just the Henry Street area. This response gives you an opportunity to sympathise with Reed.

Role actor response 5 provides you with information as to residents' perceptions. The question contained in the prompt seems to be a perfectly feasible question to ask. The information gleaned from it indeed requires you to take some form of action.

Role actor response 6 certainly requires you to react. The fact that residents are planning to take the law into their own hands has consequences not only for the residents but also for the police.

You need to be made aware of any premises in particular that are the cause of problems in the area. Role actor response 7 provides you with that information.

Role actor response 8 would be the result of you using the statistics contained in the violent crime analysis. Again the response provides you with the opportunity to offer Reed your support and reassurance.

The statistics suggest that violent crime is not just restricted to the town centre area. Role actor response 9 may sound quite dismissive but Reed does live in the town centre area and quite naturally this is the focus of their concern. However, by using the statistics relating to other areas you are trying to allay Reed's fears that it is only confined to the town centre area.

Again role actor response 10 is confrontational but at least you would have made the suggestion of working with the residents. As the article in the Castleside Chronicle does not contain the police perspective on what is occurring in the area, the press release is also worth considering.

Role actor response 11 does not offer any indication that Reed is satisfied with your suggestion. However, you have outlined your options so move on.

Assessment checklist

Competency Area	Scalar	Grade
Area 1: Effective Communication **Asks role actor:** 1.1 of incidents in the town centre/Henry Street 1.2 of problems with licensed premises 1.3 of the planned campaign	Thorough – Superficial 1 2 3 4 5	A B C D
Area 2: Planning and Organising **States intention to:** 2.1 contact council re street mess/loud music 2.2 use high visibility patrols for evenings/ early mornings at weekends 2.3 review incidents occurring at licensed premises 2.4 conduct visits to licensed premises	Clear – Unclear 1 2 3 4 5	A B C D
Area 3: Resilience **Informs role actor:** 3.1 will address concerns of residents (e.g. meeting/press/leaflets) 3.2 will monitor future conduct of licensed premises **Explains:** 3.3 not all violent crime is alcohol related 3.4 residents should not take own action 3.5 consequences of taking own action	Clear – Unclear 1 2 3 4 5	A B C D
Area 4: Community and Customer Focus **Outlines intention to:** 4.1 find out current state of Sgt Weller's initiative 4.2 work together with role actor 4.3 Reassures role actor 4.4 Outlines crime not just town centre problem	Clear – Unclear 1 2 3 4 5	A B C D
Area 5: Respect for Race and Diversity	Objective – Biased 1 2 3 4 5 Supportive – Unsupportive 1 2 3 4 5	A B C D

Assessment Checklist Debrief

The Reed exercise contains five competency areas; Problem Solving, Planning and Organising, Resilience, Community and Customer Focus and Respect for Race and Diversity.

The exercise contains 16 behavioural statements (statements a candidate should say).

We will now take each competency area and behavioural statement in turn. Have your candidate information and role actor notes to hand to see which behavioural statements you would have scored.

Area 1: Problem Solving

This area contains the minimum three behavioural statements. Notice that all are prefixed by 'Asks role actor for details'. The scalar (how well a candidate scores the behavioural statements) for this area is Thorough to Superficial.

1.1 ... of incidents in the town centre/Henry Street. You are new to the area so why not ask a person who resides in that area if they can offer you any more information about the problems being encountered by residents. It is not a sign of weakness to say to someone, "I'm new here whereas you have lived in the area for sometime. Can you give me any more information about what is happening?" or words to that affect. Asking this question would result in the delivery of role actor response 3.

1.2 ... of problems with licensed premises. As you are going to be policing the area concerned you need to be aware of all of the information relating to the problems being encountered by the residents. This question would provide you with the information contained in role actor response 7. It would then be up to you to offer suggestions as to how you intend to address the problems.

1.3 ... of the planned campaign. The first paragraph of the Castleside Chronicle article indicates that the residents have launched a campaign to highlight the problems they are facing. However, it does not provide details of what the campaign entails. You need to be aware of these details as it may require police assistance or intervention. This question would result in role actor response 6. I will address the contents of that response in due course at behavioural statement 3.5.

Area 2: Planning and Organising

This area contains four behavioural statements. Notice that all are prefixed by 'States intention to'. The scalar for this area is Clear to Unclear.

2.1 ... contact council re street mess/loud music. There is information in the newspaper article of the debris been left behind in Henry Street. Role actor response 7 indicates that loud music is also a problem. The council can be used to address both of these environmental problems. This then shows Reed that a partnership approach can be adopted to address the problems.

2.2 ... use high visibility patrols for evenings/early mornings at weekends. The use of such patrols would provide reassurance to residents. This is an everyday solution to the problem. Remember it need not just be police officers you suggest using but also Community Support Officers. The town centre notes section of the table shows that this is the time when the incidents are most frequent. Did you identify that in the candidate information?

2.3 ... review incidents occurring at licensed premises. Reviewing such incidents would give you a clearer picture of where and when the problems were occurring.

2.4 ... conduct visits to licensed premises. Visits to licensed premises would help reassure residents and help in addressing any problems in the area.

All of the options outlined in the four behavioural statements contained in this competency area are everyday options capable of being delivered by a sergeant.

Area 3: Resilience

This area contains five behavioural statements. Notice that 3.1 and 3.2 are prefixed by 'Informs role actor' and 3.3, 3.4 and 3.5 are prefixed by 'Explains'. The scalar for this area is Clear to Unclear.

3.1 ... will address concerns of residents. It is clear from the newspaper article that the residents are very concerned about the problems in the area. You need to address these concerns. This can be done in a number of ways, for example through a meeting with the residents, through the local press or through a leaflet drop in the area.

3.2 ... will monitor future conduct of licensed premises. This is another basic method of reassuring Reed and another everyday policing method. Remember it does matter in which order you score the behavioural statements. It is quite likely that you could score a number of behavioural statements in one sentence. In this exercise behavioural statements 2.3, 2.4 and 3.2 could be scored one after the other. Of course you will be unaware when undergoing the exercise that you have done this.

3.3 ... not all violent crime is alcohol related. This can be inferred from the statistics. The Bankside area has almost the same crime level as the town centre area. However, it has no alcohol related crime. The same can be said of the other three areas. The notes section of the table relating to the town centre shows that only six incidents have occurred in the public houses. The violent crime analysis document contains two notes beneath the table that you can use. The first shows that the victims of crime usually know the offender. This perhaps addresses the suggestion that residents are or will be subject to violence. The second point shows that crime does not only occurs in public houses.

3.4 ... residents should not take own actions. This should be your response to role actor response 6.

3.5 ... consequences of taking own action. Behavioural statement 3.4 should then be followed by outlining the consequences of residents taking their own action. For example, liable to arrest, putting themselves in danger or actually contributing to the disorder.

Area 4: Community and Customer Focus

This area contains four behavioural statements. Notice that 4.1 and 4.2 are prefixed by 'Outlines intention to'. The scalar for this area is Clear to Unclear.

4.1 ... find out current state of Sgt Weller's initiative. Sergeant Weller's initiative is mentioned in Inspector Tait's memorandum. Mentioning this to Reed would indicate that the police do take the problem seriously. This would address Reed's comments in the newspaper article.

4.2 ... work together with role actor. You want to work with the residents not against them. This would be of benefit to all.

4.3 Reassures role actor. The residents are dissatisfied with what they perceive as the lack of police action in relation to the problems in the area. You need to reassure Reed that the police do intend to tackle the problem

4.4 Outlines that crime is not just town centre problem. This information can be drawn from the statistics as I outlined at behavioural statement 3.3.

Area 5: Respect for Race and Diversity
This competency area does not contain behavioural statements. You are assessed across the five-minute interaction against two scalars, in this case Objective to Biased and Supportive to Unsupportive.

It is essential to maintain a balanced view when dealing with the exercises. This is relevant to both police and non-police exercises.

Candidate instructions

In this exercise you will have two pages of preparatory information:

- a memorandum from Inspector Tait
- a memorandum from C Ling, Force Communication Centre

During the activity phase you will meet A Sher.

CASTLESHIRE POLICE

Memorandum

From:	Inspector Tait, Castleside
To:	Sergeant 'Candidate', team 5, Castleside
Subject:	Meeting with A Sher
Date:	yesterday

I'm sorry that I am not able to welcome you in person on your first day but I have to attend a Community Safety Strategy meeting at headquarters.

A Sher of 22 Castle View, Castleside, has contacted the station and requested a meeting with a senior officer. They would only tell the call-taker that it was in relation to an incident at their home.

I have no idea what this meeting is about. However, I have requested a copy of the call log for 22 Castle View, which is attached. I have not spoken with Constable Howard, team 5 as he has been on a driving course over the past week.

In my absence I would like you to meet with A Sher. I look forward to meeting with you later upon my return to the station.

L Tait

Inspector

CASTLESHIRE POLICE

Memorandum

From:	C Ling, Force Communication Centre
To:	Inspector Tait, Castleside
Subject:	22 Castle View, Castleside – Call log enquiry
Date:	yesterday

Please find below the results of your request for information in relation to 22 Castle View, Castleside.

Date	Time	Informant	Information
Thursday, two weeks ago	*22.20*	*A Sher* *22 Castle View* *Castleside* *Tel: 01803 832245*	*Report of damage to motor vehicle. Informant requesting to speak to officer.*

Date	Time	Officer	Action
Thursday, two weeks ago	*22.22*	*PC 1128 Howard*	*Officer en route*
Thursday, two weeks ago	*22.30*	*PC 1128 Howard*	*Officer at scene*
Thursday, two weeks ago	*22.50*	*PC 1128 Howard*	*Details obtained for crime report. Advice given, no suspects.*
Thursday, two weeks ago	*22.55*		*Log closed*

C Ling

C Ling

Candidate information debrief

I have mentioned previously that you should not try and second-guess or pre-empt the content or issues contained in an exercise until you have read all of the candidate information. However, on occasion you can read through an exercise in your preparatory phase and have an inkling about what an exercise may be regarding. For example, the Reed exercise in this book is clearly about residents' concerns surrounding disorder and anti-social behaviour, it states as much in the newspaper article.

The Sher exercise is not like this and has been designed to give you experience of reading through an exercise, and then considering what it is about. What are the issues? As you will see when we debrief the candidate information, there is no indication as to what the issues may be and you will have to use the role actor as your main source of information.

Memorandum from Inspector Tait

The opening paragraph outlines that Inspector Tait is unable to meet Sher as they have had to attend a meeting at force headquarters.

The next paragraph points out that Sher contacted Castleside Police Station requesting a meeting with a senior officer, so be prepared to deal with that expectation. Intriguingly, they would not inform the call-taker why they were requesting the meeting. The result of this is that you have no indication as to what Sher wants to discuss.

The next paragraph merely outlines to you the fact that an incident occurred at Sher's home, 22 Castle View and that Constable Howard attended. Constable Howard has been on a driving course for the past week. Is that significant to the exercise?

Memorandum from C Ling

This memorandum contains a call log relating to Sher's address.

But what does it tell you? An incident of damage to a motor vehicle occurred two weeks ago. Is the date or offence significant?

Constable Howard attended within 10 minutes and took a crime report. The call log was endorsed with the information 'advice given, no suspects'. The call log was closed 35 minutes after the original call was made. So there is still no indication as to why Sher has requested the meeting.

What were your first thoughts on reading the candidate information?

Obviously there is little or no indication as to what the issues may be. You can speculate but may be wide of the mark. It is far better to seek clarification from the person with all the answers – the role actor.

Role actor instructions

You are Andrew/Audrey Sher. You are gay. You work as an office manager and live at 22 Castle View, Castleside with your partner Michael/Michelle. You moved to the area three months ago having bought the property with your partner. The house is in a terrace, which is in an area mostly owned by housing associations.

On Thursday, two weeks ago, your car was vandalised by unknown persons who broke the wiper blades and scratched the bonnet. Constable Tim Howard attended and obtained details for a crime report. You were most impressed with the officer, in that he arrived promptly and appeared genuinely concerned and helpful. He also gave you his direct dial voicemail number and said if you had any further problems to contact this number.

On Monday last week, a packet of flour was poured over your car and the word 'Queers' written in it. You rang the direct dial number and left a message for Constable Howard. Two days later, your rubbish bin had been emptied in your front garden. You again rang the number and left a message. On neither occasion has Constable Howard returned your calls.

The latest incident occurred yesterday morning when you went downstairs in the morning to find dog excrement had been put through your letterbox. You believe these incidents are occurring because of your sexuality. You have no witnesses to the incidents. You rang Castleside Police Station and asked to speak to the person in charge but were told there was no one available. As a result you said you would attend the station the next day and asked that the Inspector be informed.

Demeanour: annoyed and frustrated

When you enter the room, say:

1. **"I'm Andrew/Audrey Sher. I was at least expecting to see the Inspector."**

   If the candidate asks what you want out of the meeting/why they want the meeting, say:

2. **"My partner and I are being repeatedly harassed and you're doing nothing to sort it out."**

   If the candidate asks what you mean by repeatedly harassed, say:

3. "Since having our car damaged, there have been three further incidents."

If the candidate asks for details of the further incidents, say:

4. "Last Monday we had flour emptied over the car and 'Queers' written in it. Then the rubbish bin was emptied in the garden and yesterday morning, dog excrement was put through the letter box."

If the candidate asks why you haven't reported these incidents, say:

5. "Constable Howard said to ring his direct dial voicemail if anything else happened. I've left two messages but have heard nothing."

If the candidate asks what Constable Howard did when he attended initial incident, say:

6. "Constable Howard just took details but he appeared genuinely concerned and very helpful towards my partner and I."

If the candidate asks if you wish to make a complaint regarding Constable Howard, say:

7. "No, I just want these incidents to stop."

If the candidate states the incidents are hate crime/outlines force policy for dealing with hate crime, say:

8. "Thank you Sergeant. I appreciate you taking these matters seriously."

If the candidate states they will arrange to take details of all the incidents, say:

9. "That would be a start. I just want the harassment to stop."

If the candidate asks if you know who is responsible, say:

10. "The boy next door has made a few comments when I've been leaving the house with my partner. But I don't have anything concrete."

If the candidate asks for details about the comments, say:

11. "I can't remember anything in particular. They are just childish remarks about gays."

If the candidate apologises for the police response, say:

12. "I am sorry that I have had to come to the station but we can't be expected to put up with this."

Role actor instructions debrief

The candidate information gives little or no indication as to what the issues are in this exercise. Therefore, I want to approach the role actor instructions debrief in a different way to the method we have used in the previous exercises.

I will not debrief the role actor instructions background but approach it as if the assessment centre buzzer has just sounded and Sher has entered your room. You are still unsure as to what the issues are in the exercise.

As I mentioned in the candidate information debrief, Sher has indicated that they were expecting to meet with Inspector Tait. You know, from the candidate information, that Inspector Tait is at a meeting at force headquarters. Consequently, you have informed Sher of this fact.

You ask Sher what they want from the meeting or why they have asked for the meeting; remember there is no indication in the candidate information. You are provided with role actor response 2.

You should follow this up by asking what Sher means by repeatedly harassed. You receive role actor response 3.

By listening to what the role actor is saying, you should realise that you need to ask for details of the three further incidents. This will prompt role actor response 4. You now have one of the issues contained in this exercise. How would you react to that information? Clearly you are now dealing with an incident of hate crime.

However, if you recall from Inspector Tait's memorandum, the only call logged for Sher's address was the incident that Constable Howard attended. So why hasn't Sher reported the other incidents?

Asking that question would result in you receiving role actor response 5. This is another example of how to link information from your two sources. Sher states that they called Constable Howard last Monday and left subsequent messages on the officer's direct dial voicemail. However, if you recall Inspector Tait's memorandum, Constable Howard has been on a driving course over the past week. Consequently, they have not have received Sher's messages. Sher is now of the opinion that the police do not care about the incidents.

Role actor response 6 eliminates any suspicion that Constable Howard was acting in a homophobic manner. In fact, it is quite the contrary. The role actor instructions provide further information as to how helpful Constable Howard was when he attended the scene.

Role actor response 7 clearly states that Sher does not want to complain about Constable Howard. There would be no point in pursuing this any further. Sher has made their feelings known as regards any complaint against Constable Howard.

Role actor response 8 would result in outlining that Castleshire Police has a hate crime policy and that such incidents are taken seriously. This would reassure Sher that the incidents would be investigated.

The incidents require investigation, so inform Sher that an investigation will take place. Role actor response 9 would result.

Sher may already know, or have a suspicion, who is responsible. Role actor response 10 provides you with that information.

The follow up question would be to clarify exactly what the boy's comments were. Role actor response 11 would indicate that the boy is aware of Sher's sexuality. That could be a starting point for any subsequent investigation.

Listen to the role actor and respond accordingly. Ask the correct questions and you will receive the information you require to address the issues.

Assessment checklist

Competency Area	Scalar	Grade
Area 1: Community and Customer Focus **Informs role actor:** 1.1 they will keep them updated re investigation 1.2 Constable Howard on driving course. 1.3 Apologises for poor/lack of police service	Clear – Unclear 1 2 3 4 5	A B C D
Area 2: Effective Communication **Asks role actor for details:** 2.1 of Constable Howard's actions at scene 2.2 about subsequent incidents 2.3 of any witnesses 2.4 of comments by neighbour 2.5 of who may be responsible for incidents	Thorough – Superficial 1 2 3 4 5	A B C D
Area 3: Problem Solving **Informs role actor:** 3.1 of intent to speak to Constable Howard 3.2 all incidents will be recorded/investigated. 3.3 Advises role actor to contact the Communications Centre direct re further incidents	Clear – Unclear 1 2 3 4 5	A B C D
Area 4: Resilience **Informs role actor:** 4.1 incidents amount to hate crime 4.2 of hate crime policy/take incidents seriously 4.3 will update Inspector Tait about meeting	Clear – Unclea 1 2 3 4 5	A B C D
Area 5: Respect for Race and Diversity	Objective – Biased 1 2 3 4 5 Sensitive – Insensitive 1 2 3 4 5	A B C D

Assessment checklist debrief

The Sher exercise contains five competency areas; Community and Customer Focus, Effective Communication, Problem Solving, Resilience and Respect for Race and Diversity.

The exercise contains 14 behavioural statements (statements a candidate should say). Remember, there will be no more than six and no less than three behavioural statements in a competency area. Respect for Race and Diversity does not contain behavioural statements.

We will now take each competency area and behavioural statement in turn. Have your candidate information and role actor notes to hand to see which behavioural statements you would have scored.

Area 1: Community and Customer Focus
This area contains the minimum three behavioural statements. Notice that all are prefixed by 'Informs role actor'. The scalar (how well a candidate scores the behavioural statements) for this area is Clear to Unclear.

1.1 ... they will keep them updated re the investigation. Sher considers that the police have ignored the two previous calls made to Constable Howard. You need to build up trust in the police. Suggesting that you keep them updated will go some way towards doing this. It is also worth considering that if you were a victim of crime you would expect to be appraised of the investigation.

1.2 Constable Howard on driving course. Explaining that Constable Howard was on a driving course will provide the reason as to why Sher's calls were not returned.

1.3 Apologises for poor/lack of police service. Apologising for poor service is not a sign of weakness. Although not intentional, Sher has received poor treatment.

Area 2: Effective Communication
This area contains five behavioural statements. Notice that all are prefixed by 'Asks role actor for details'. The scalar for this area is Thorough to Superficial.

2.1 ... of Constable Howard's actions at scene. You need this information to ascertain the standard of Constable Howard's performance at the incident. Role actor response 6 would be the result.

2.2 ... about subsequent incidents. This question could be asked after receiving role actor response 3. Role actor response 4 would provide you with the information.

2.3 ... of any witnesses. You need this information if the police are to investigate the incidents. The fact that Sher has no witnesses is contained in the role actor instructions.

2.4 ... of comments by neighbour. This question is the follow up to receiving role actor response 10. Role actor response 11 provides you with the information.

2.5 ... of who may be responsible for incidents. As you intend to have the incidents investigated, asking Sher relevant questions would be pertinent. Role actor response 10 would result.

All of the questions in this competency area help you to build up a picture of what has occurred and help inform you as to how you intend to progress with the matter.

Area 3: Problem Solving
This area contains the minimum three behavioural statements. Notice that all are prefixed by 'Informs role actor'. The scalar for this area is Clear to Unclear.

3.1 ... of intent to speak to Constable Howard. You are Constable Howard's supervisor and you must do this. This may be to clarify details of the incident or to point out that leaving his direct dial voicemail as a point of contact is not suitable.

3.2 ... all incidents will be recorded/investigated. Apart from the original incident two weeks ago, the other incidents are not yet recorded and need to be investigated. Suggesting either recording or investigating would score this behavioural statement. Suggesting both would achieve a higher scalar for this behavioural statement.

3.3 Advises role actor to contact the communications centre direct re further incidents. Suggesting this would avoid the problems caused by leaving messages on an officer's direct dial voicemail. Calling the communications centre direct would also ensure a speedier response.

Area 4: Resilience

This area contains the minimum three behavioural statements. Notice that all are prefixed by 'Informs role actor'. The scalar for this area is Clear to Unclear.

4.1 ... incidents amount to hate crime. Although not contained in the candidate information, it is something of which you should be aware.

4.2 ... of hate cvime policy/take incidents seriously. Your own force will no doubt have a hate crime policy. Castleside Police certainly does. Before attending your actual assessment centre you will receive a document referred to as a divisional profile. This document contains policies referring to the force in which the assessment centre is located. These are the policies you need to be aware of.

4.3 ... will update Inspector Tait about meeting. Sher originally contacted the police and requested to speak to a senior officer. Outlining to Sher that you will update Inspector Tait shows that the police do take the problem seriously.

Area 5: Respect for Race and Diversity

This competency area does not contain behavioural statements. You are assessed across the five-minute interaction against two scalars, in this case Objective to Biased and Sensitive to Insensitive. You should not be biased towards the police and you should be sensitive to Sher's situation.

Although Sher may be a member of the gay community, the Respect for Race and Diversity competency area would not carry any more weight in the assessment process.

Candidate instructions

In this exercise you will receive four pages of preparatory information:

- a memorandum from Inspector Tait
- a copy of an email from Constable Ali
- two incident reports

During the activity phase you will meet S Todd.

CASTLESHIRE POLICE

Memorandum

From: Inspector Tait, Castleside
To: Sergeant 'Candidate', team 5, Castleside
Subject: Illegal Encampment
Date: today

Three days ago a group of travellers arrived on a piece of council owned land adjacent to Castle Park. This area contains an exclusive golf course, hotel and approximately 20 residential properties. There is a footpath, which runs through the area where the travellers are encamped that leads onto to the Castle Park development.

Our gypsy and traveller liaison officer has visited the site and liased with the local council, who will, in the next few days, be serving notice on the travellers requiring them to leave the land. However, tensions in the area have been rising. The local community has been voicing its discontent, congregating in the area on an evening with video cameras filming the travellers. I am concerned that the behaviour may antagonise an incident of disorder. I have arranged for you to meet S Todd, one of the residents who has become a self-appointed spokes person.

For your information I have attached a report from the gypsy and traveller liaison officer and details of two incidents that have been reported by the local residents.

L Tait

Inspector

Email Printout

From: Constable Ali, Castleside gypsy traveller liaison officer
To: Inspector Tait, Castleside
Date: yesterday
Subject: Traveller Encampment at Castle Park Golf Course and Estate

Inspector,

I am visiting the site on a daily basis. Today I visited with a health visitor who has arranged immunisation injections for the children. Arrangements have also been made for the children to attend the local school tomorrow. The travellers are running a paving business and have a number of contracts in the Castleside area.

At 3.30 pm this afternoon I accompanied the borough council officers who informed the Travellers that a case would be put before Castleside County Court with a view to a repossession order being granted in order to have them evicted from the land. I discussed with the council officers the provision of sanitary arrangements, water and the removal of rubbish during the interim time whilst this order was being obtained. These facilities will be provided.

Whilst at Castle Park I also spoke to S Todd, a resident of the Castle Park Estate, who was very vocal about the situation. During the conversation there was mention that there would be a residents meeting, which most of the residents would be likely to attend. S Todd was concerned that the travellers would find out about the meeting and that they would attend with a view to disrupting the meeting. Consequently, as feelings are running high at the moment, disorder may result.

Adam Ali

Gypsy traveller liaison officer

Incident reports

Incident No:	679
Time/Date:	4:45, 2 days ago
Location:	Castle Park Drive, Castleside
Informant:	S Todd, 18 Castle Park Drive, Castle Park, Castleside
Tel:	077855 323458
Description:	A large group of travellers are smashing up a vehicle on the council land at the rear of Castle Park Golf Course
14:50	CA45 despatched
14:51	TA55 despatched
14:51	CA43 despatched
14:55	Further call received from Tony Braithwaite at number 16 Castle Park Drive
15:00	CA45 arrived
15:01	From CA45 no further patrols required, no disturbance taking place
15:30	From CA45 PC 877 I have spoken to the owner of the vehicle Andrew Lenkavich. He has been working for the travellers delivering leaflets and when calling to collect his wages there has been a dispute during which time his car sustained minor damaged. He does not want to make a complaint. Advice given.

Incident No:	872
Time/Date:	18:45, yesterday
Location:	Castle Park Drive, Castleside
Informant:	Mrs Brooks, 5 Castle Park Drive, Castle Park, Castleside
Tel:	01273 566811
Description:	The travellers have stolen my nine-year-old son's bike
19:10	CA55 despatched
19:30	CA55 arrived
20:35	From CA55 PC 2548 the bike has not been stolen. A group of local children have been playing with some of the traveller's children and the bike was left behind. It has been found and returned to the owner. This is not a crime.

Candidate information debrief

This is the third and final non-police exercise in the series of seven. The traditional composition of the seven exercises in the actual assessment centre is four police exercises and three non-police exercises. The seven in this book have reflected that composition.

How did you get on with the Todd exercise? Although the exercise front cover informs you that you have four pages of candidate information you will now appreciate that two of the four pages are incidents reports that do not take very long to read. However, both contain relevant information for you to use in your meeting with Todd.

Should an exercise contain three or four pages of candidate information, do not be tempted to have a glance to see what the length these documents are. You are wasting your precious time. Far better to get on and read the candidate information in order. Remember, the rigorous exercise design process ensures that you have time to read through the candidate information.

Memorandum from Inspector Tait

The opening paragraph sets the scene for you. A group of travellers have arrived on council owned land adjacent to an exclusive housing and hotel development.

The local council, and force gypsy and traveller liaison officer, have visited the site. The travellers will soon be served with a notice to quit the land. This is useful piece of information for you to use during your meeting with Todd.

More alarmingly for the police, is the fact that tensions have been rising and the local residents have been filming the travellers. Inspector Tait is concerned that the residents' actions may result in disorder. You too should share those concerns. S Todd is the self-appointed spokesperson.

Inspector Tait has attached a report from the force gypsy and traveller liaison officer and details of two incidents that have been reported by the residents.

I'm sure that you will agree that unlike the Sher exercise, it is clear what the main issue is in this exercise.

Email from Constable Ali, gypsy and traveller liaison officer

The first paragraph contains some very useful information for you.

Particularly the fact that Constable Ali is visiting the site daily (notice that this information is contained in only a few words at the beginning of the email) and arrangements have been made for the children to attend the local school.

Paragraph 2 also contains information for you to use during your meeting with Todd. Namely, the council are seeking a repossession order for the land, rubbish will be removed and sanitary arrangements will be provided.

The final paragraph explains that the residents are planning a meeting where most are likely to attend. The residents are concerned that the travellers will disrupt their meeting and disorder may result. What notes did you make in relation to this meeting? What police action did you consider? You are the sergeant now you must decide what action you are going to take.

Incident reports
Both incident reports contain valuable information for you to use when meeting Todd. However, I will cover this information when we debrief the assessment checklist behavioural statements.

Role actor instructions

You are Stephen/Stephanie Todd. You and your partner are both doctors at the local hospital. Neither of you have any children. You moved to Castle Park last year and paid a considerable amount of money for your home, which is one of a number of executive houses. All the residents have membership of the championship golf course, which is part of the Castle Park development.

The travellers are staying on a piece of land that is directly behind many of the houses on Castle Park Drive. You and other residents are worried that the value of your homes will decrease if the travellers stay or regularly return to this piece of land. The travellers are encamped on a grassed area that has a public footpath crossing it leading to the fields behind. There are a number of pleasant walking routes, which lead around the area and across the golf course. You and other residents use these footpaths to walk your dogs. The travellers' caravans are parked around the route of the footpath and you have found it intimidating when you have tried to walk through them.

You are concerned about the amount of rubbish that will build up on the traveller's site and have already noticed a pile of rubbish bags developing. The house closest to where the travellers are staying is yours and so you have taken it upon yourself to take action. You have been video recording the travellers and going round speaking to other residents in an attempt to form a residents' group. You have booked a room at the local village hall for a meeting. This is planned for tomorrow night.

You are unaware the gypsy and traveller liaison officer is attending the site.

Demeanour: concerned and annoyed

When you enter the room, say:

1. **"Hello sergeant I'm Stephen/Stephanie Todd. I want to know what the police are going to do to get rid of these travellers."**

   If the candidate asks what problems you are having with the Travellers, say:

2. "They are causing a mess on the land next to our homes, and when we are trying to walk the footpath we are mobbed by their filthy kids. I find it quite intimidating."

If the candidate asks what you mean by 'mobbed' or 'intimidated', say:

3. "The travellers are all over the footpath and it is stopping us walking our dogs that way."

If the candidate asks you for further details, say:

4. "This is affecting our lives and the value of our homes. There are rubbish bags being left right outside my garden."

If the candidate says the rubbish is a council problem or that they will speak to the council about this, say:

5. "That might sort that problem but what about all the crimes that are happening. There have been two already since their arrival."

If the candidate asks what you know about the incidents of crime, say:

6. "I saw a car being damaged and I know a bike was stolen from outside number five."

If the candidate explains the bike was not stolen, say:

7. "Well at least the police did something about that report."

If the candidate asks what you mean by that comment or what happened after the report of the car being damaged, say:

8. "I reported it to the police but no one called to see me."

If the candidate asks what you saw about the damage, say:

9. "There was a lot of noise and I saw at least one kick the car but I couldn't identify which one."

If the candidate asks what has been organised by the residents or what is planned at the residents meeting, say:

10. "We all feel very strongly about the travellers and are getting together to work out what we can do to get rid of them, since the council and police do not seem to be bothered."

If the candidate states that the travellers will be given notice to leave the land by the council, say:

11. "That cannot come soon enough."

If the candidate asks why you think there will be trouble at the meeting from the travellers, say:

12. **"I expect it's the sort of thing their type would do."**

If the candidate suggests that the police or the council will attend the residents meeting, say:

13. **"Good, it's about time you saw our point of view."**

If the candidate states that the police role is to be impartial or warns about any illegal action by the residents, say:

14. **"I understand, but we will be pressing for action by the local council."**

If the candidate outlines what the police will do to visit the site or co-ordinate action, say:

15. **"I only hope that improves things for the residents."**

Role actor instructions debrief

As with all of the exercises in the series, the Todd exercise is not an issue of gender. The opening paragraph of the role actor instructions outlines the details contained in the candidate information relating to the Castle Park development.

The second paragraph outlines Todd's concerns in relation to the value of their property being diminished should the travellers stay or regularly return to the piece of land. Todd has found the travellers' presence intimidating. Is Todd's main concern the effect on the value of their property?

The residents are planning to take action and have organised a meeting at a local village hall.

Todd's demeanour is concerned and annoyed.

The opening role actor response does suggest a confrontational tone in Todd's manner. Do not be fazed by this, continue to focus on your candidate information notes.

Role actor response 2 clearly outlines Todd's views of the travellers.

Todd has mentioned in role actor response 2 that people are being 'mobbed' and 'intimidated' by the travellers. Seeking clarification about this would result in the delivery of role actor response 3.

You need to build up a picture and obtain as much detail as possible so a follow up question of, 'What else can you tell me?' would result in role actor response 4.

You need to start reassuring Todd. Todd mentioned in role actor response 4 that rubbish is accumulating. This can be tackled by the council. However, role actor response 5 contains a perception by Todd that the travellers are responsible for crime in the area.

Role actor response 6 outlines Todd's perception of the crimes committed by the travellers. This response would provide you with the opportunity to refer to the information contained in the two incident reports.

Role actor response 7 does require a reaction from you. What does Todd mean by that remark? Role actor response 8 provides you with that information. You will need to respond to that comment. I will cover that in the assessment checklist debrief.

Role actor response 9 is interesting for you as a candidate. Not only does it indicate that Todd witnessed the incident, it indicates that they could not identify the person responsible. If they could identify the person you would feel obliged to take details as it is evidence of first description which would take up a lot of your five minutes.

Role actor response 10 provides you with details of the residents' meeting. You need to be aware of this as you may have to put in place police resources to prevent or deal with any disorder.

You need to reassure Todd that action has been taken to remove the travellers. Role actor response 11 would result. Remember though, you must remain impartial.

Role actor response 12 certainly needs a response from you for there is no indication that this is the case. In fact the candidate information gives no indication whatsoever that the travellers have caused any disorder. There are certainly no reports that this is the case. The two reported incidents do not indicate that the travellers have been targeting the residents.

Role actor response 13 provides you with an opportunity to outline that the police are impartial in these matters.

Should you do this, role actor response 14 would result. The delivery of this response would provide you with an opportunity to point out that the council have applied for a repossession order for the land.

Role actor response 15 could be delivered when you have outlined that the gypsy and traveller liaison officer will be visiting the site daily and/or the police are working in conjunction with the council.

Although the role actor responses are printed in a specific order this is for the benefit of the role actor. Regardless of which point in the five-minute interaction you ask a question or make a comment, the role actor will provide you with the relevant response.

Assessment checklist

Competency Area	Scalar	Grade
Area 1: Problem Solving **Asks role actor:** 1.1 for details of vehicle being damaged 1.2 for details of the residents' meeting/ planned actions. 1.3 Outlines an officer should have spoken to role actor about the damage to the vehicle	Thorough – Superficial 1 2 3 4 5	A B C D
Area 2: Planning and Organising **States:** 2.1 will attend residents' meeting 2.2 will contact the council for the date when the notice will be served 2.3 gypsy traveller liaison officer will visit the site each day	Thorough – Superficial 1 2 3 4 5	A B C D
Area 3: Community and Customer Focus **Informs role actor:** 3.1 will find out the council plans for removal of rubbish/provision of sanitation 3.2 will explain to residents what has been arranged/what can be done to remove the travellers from the land **Explains:** 3.3 that the bike was not stolen 3.4 details of damage to car incident 3.5 residents must not take own action 3.6 police role is to be impartial	Clear – Unclear 1 2 3 4 5	A B C D
Area 4: Respect for Race and Diversity	Objective – Biased 1 2 3 4 5 Sensitive – Insensitive 1 2 3 4 5	A B C D

Assessment checklist debrief

The Todd exercise contains four competency areas; Problem Solving, Planning and Organising, Community and Customer Focus, and Respect for Race and Diversity.

The exercise contains 12 behavioural statements (statements a candidate should say). This is the minimum number allowed in an exercise assessment checklist. Remember there will be no more than six and no less than three behavioural statements in a competency area. Respect for Race and Diversity does not contain behavioural statements.

We will now take each competency area and behavioural statement in turn. Have your candidate information and role actor notes to hand to see which behavioural statements you would have scored.

Area 1: Problem Solving
This area contains the minimum three behavioural statements. Notice that 1.1 and 1.2 are prefixed by 'Asks role actor'. The scalar (how well a candidate scores the behavioural statements) for this area is Thorough to Superficial.

1.1 ... for details of vehicle being damaged. If you refer to the incident log regarding the damage to the vehicle, you will see that Todd was the caller. Although the vehicle owner does not wish to make a complaint, does Todd have any further information? Todd reported the vehicle being 'smashed up' but the officer attending found only minor damage. Role actor response 9 provides you with the information.

1.2 ... for details of the residents' meeting/planned actions. You need this information to plan a potential police response. Asking such questions as when and/or where the meeting will take place or how many people will be attending will provide you with the information you require. Role actor response 10 also provides you with information.

1.3 Outlines an officer should have spoken to role actor about the damage to the vehicle. This should be your response to role actor response 8. An officer should have updated Todd of the incident result.

Area 2: Planning and Organising
This area contains the minimum three behavioural statements. Notice that all are prefixed by 'States'. The scalar for this area is Thorough to

Superficial.

2.1 ... will attend residents' meeting. You need to do this to start building up trust with the residents and to try and defuse any potential conflict.

2.2 ... will contact the council for the date when the notice will be served. The council have applied for a repossession order. Providing Todd with timescales when the travellers will move from the site will go someway towards allaying their concerns and may even prevent potential conflict.

2.3 ... gypsy and traveller liaison officer will visit the site each day. Todd is unaware of this fact. This would show that the police are interested in the problems the residents feel they have and that the police are assisting the travellers.

Area 3: Community and Customer Focus

This area contains five behavioural statements. Notice that 3.1 and 3.2 are prefixed by 'Informs role actor' and 3.3, 3.4 and 3.5 prefixed by 'Explains'. The scalar for this area is Clear to Unclear.

3.1 ... will find out the council plans for removal of rubbish/provision of sanitation. This behavioural statement is similar to 2.3 in that you are providing reassurance to Todd.

3.2 ... will explain to residents what has been arranged/what can be done to remove the travellers from the land. This behavioural statement could link to 2.1. It explains what you intend to do when you attend the meeting.

3.3 ... that the bike was not stolen. This behavioural statement can be scored by responding to role actor response 6. You are using the information contained in the incident reports to address Todd's perception of the crime he believes the travellers are committing. The bicycle was not stolen and the damage to the car was the result of a dispute with someone the travellers were employing. In neither case was a resident the victim of a crime.

3.4 ... details of damage to car incident. See notes for behavioural statement 3.3

3.5 ... residents must not take own action. You must point this out to Todd. Outlining the potential consequences would achieve a higher scalar for this behavioural statement. Outlining that Todd should not video record the travellers would also fall into this behavioural statement.

3.6 ... police role is to be impartial. This is a response to role actor responses 12 and 13 which could be pointed out at the start of the five-minute interaction. Stating 'The police do not take sides' would be sufficient to score this behavioural statement.

Area 4: Respect for Race and Diversity
As I previously mentioned this competency area does not contain behavioural statements. You are assessed across the five-minute interaction against two scalars, in this case Objective to Biased and Sensitive to Insensitive.

Throughout the five-minute interaction you should remain objective towards both parties and sensitive to the needs of the residents and the travellers.

INSPECTOR EXERCISE
ALSTON

Candidate instructions

In this exercise you will receive two pages of preparatory information:

- a memorandum from Chief Inspector Venerdi
- a memorandum from Inspector Kerr

During the activity phase you will meet Sergeant P Alston.

CASTLESHIRE POLICE

Memorandum

From: Chief Inspector Venerdi, Castleside
To: Inspector 'Candidate', Castleside
Subject: Custody Sergeant P Alston
Date: yesterday

I have received the attached report from Inspector Kerr who is responsible for Administration of Justice Department. It concerns performance issues relating to Sergeant P Alston. The officer has been a permanent custody sergeant for the last year.

At Castleside there are designated custody sergeants, although the role is an important one for the division, it is not a popular posting. Sergeant Alston was promoted into this role in order to fill a vacancy. There is a one year tenure associated with the posting. Prior to promotion, Sergeant Alston worked for more than 10 years as a specialist roads policing officer and was well thought of. Just prior to their promotion, the officer completed a period of acting in the division as a uniform sergeant and received good reports from the Inspector.

I am not aware of any other performance issues for the sergeant and so would like you to address the points raised by Inspector Kerr as you see fit. Therefore, I have asked Sergeant Alston to meet you on your first day.

L Venerdi

Chief Inspector Venerdi

CASTLESHIRE POLICE

Memorandum

From:	Inspector Kerr, Administration of Justice Department
To:	Chief Inspector Venerdi, Castleside
Subject:	Custody Sergeant P Alston
Date:	two days ago

In my current role as the Administration of Justice Manager at Castleside, two issues concerning Custody Sergeant Alston have come to my attention.

Incident 1:

This refers to the detainee John Morrison, aged 15 years, who was arrested on 18th of last month for aggravated vehicle taking. Constable James was the investigating officer. Following interview, Constable James wished to arrest Morrison's mother for attempting to pervert the course of justice as part of the investigation. Sergeant Alston refused to accept Morrison's mother into custody if arrested and stated Morrison would be bailed. Any later enquiry after Morrison was released from custody would be contaminated due to contact between Morrison and his mother.

Incident 2:

This incident refers to the detainee Chantelle Gold, aged 27 years, who was arrested for Shoplifting on 17th of last month. Gold was charged and bailed with conditions to Castleside Magistrates' court on 30th of last month. Sergeant Alston imposed the bail condition of 'NOT TO STEAL ANYTHING FROM ANYWHERE'. Although bail conditions were appropriate as Gold was identified as a prolific offender the condition imposed was unprofessional and certainly would have reflected badly in court.

The incidents have not been investigated and I believe, subject to your agreement, can be addressed at a local level.

S Kerr

Inspector Kerr

Candidate information debrief

This is the first exercise in your series of seven. The seven exercises will reflect the traditional exercise composition of the actual Part II assessment centre; four police exercises (where you meet a member of the police organisation) and three non-police exercises (where you meet a member of the public).

Memorandum from Chief Inspector Venerdi

The opening paragraph outlines that a report has been received from Inspector Kerr, Administration of Justice Department, concerning the performance of Sergeant Alston. Sergeant Alston has been a custody sergeant for the last year. At this point do not try to second guess or pre-empt the issues contained in an exercise. Clearly Sergeant Alston's performance is an issue but that is the only information you have at present. Perhaps they have performed well and Inspector Kerr's memorandum is complimentary.

The second paragraph of the memorandum provides you with some background to the custody sergeant role. Worthy of note for you as the divisional Inspector is that the role is not viewed as a popular posting.

Sergeant Alston was promoted into the role, which is subject to a one-year tenure. The memorandum informed you that Alston has been in the role for the last year. Is this significant to the exercise?

Alston spent 10 years as a roads policing officer and just prior to promotion successfully completed a period of acting sergeant within the division.

Chief Inspector Venerdi is not aware of any performance issues relating to Alston and leaves you to decide how best to deal with Alston.

No doubt by now you will be anticipating that Alston has under performed in some area of their work.

Memorandum from Inspector Kerr

The memorandum contains a lot of information for you to work through, particularly on serious performance issues on the part of Alston. Issues that you, as the divisional Inspector will have to address.

At this point in the first exercise of the series I want to stress to you the importance of taking on the role of an Inspector when working through these exercises. The Part II assessment centre is designed to assess your potential to perform in the rank of Inspector. It is therefore essential that you get into this role. Failure to do so will result in you not addressing the issues contained in the exercises.

Returning to the Alston exercise, what notes did you make in relation to the two incidents outlined in Inspector Kerr's memorandum? You should have picked up on the fact that Alston's actions on both occasions were unprofessional and unacceptable. However, did you make notes relating to the consequences of their actions or to enquire why the incidents occurred? When completing the exercises you need to always bear in mind the consequences of someone's actions or their failure to act and to consider why someone has acted in the way described in the exercise. There is always a reason. If it doesn't state the reason in the candidate information then your other source of information, the role actor, will have it.

I will refer to the information contained in the two incident reports when we debrief the assessment checklist.

Role actor instructions

You are Sergeant Patrick/Patricia Alston. You have 14 years' service, 10 years of which you have spent in specialist traffic posts working on both motorway and divisional duties. You regard yourself as an experienced traffic investigator. You were promoted to sergeant a year ago. Just before your promotion you spent a period acting as a uniform patrol sergeant. You thoroughly enjoyed this role, receiving good feedback from your inspector and staff who were disappointed that you were not promoted within the post.

In Castleshire Police, when applying for promotion you are required to say that you are willing to work anywhere in the force area. The role of custody sergeant is the one you least wanted to perform. It is a very unpopular posting and due to difficulties in getting sergeants to fill vacancies, the Castleshire Police has recently started to promote officers into custody sergeant posts. You were asked to take on the post of custody sergeant at Castleside and because you were concerned of the consequences of not accepting agreed to the role.

You have found that you have been able to quickly learn the role and now feel confident in your responsibilities. However, due to staff shortage because of long term sickness, you have over the last two months been required to work longer shifts and on rest days. Also, when on duty you are rarely able to find time to eat or have a break during a shift that can be from 10 to 12 hours in length. You have begun to feel constantly tired and demotivated, as you can see no end to the situation. You are beginning to think your specialist skills are wasted in custody and can see no opportunities arising to perform a patrol or traffic sergeant role.

You are aware the custody officer post is subject to a one-year tenure but you have had no indication that you will be moved following completion of your year. In fact you do not believe this will happen as there are custody sergeants similar to you who were promoted into the post and have been there for well in excess of their year.

Demeanour: confident but despondent.

When you enter the room, say:

1. **"Hello inspector, I'm Sergeant Pat Alston. The chief inspector said you need to see me"**

    If the candidate asks why you stated you would bail Morrison and refused to accept his mother in custody, say.

2.	"It had been a busy day. I thought Constable James was making the investigation overly complex. There was only one free cell and I did not want cell space taken up in case another prisoner arrived."

If the candidate asks if you gave Gold the bail condition 'NOT TO STEAL ANYTHING FROM ANYWHERE', say.

3.	"I probably did, thought I might as well cover all the bases."

If the candidate points out you made incorrect/poor decisions or the consequences of the decisions, say:

4.	"That's as may be, but it was my decision at the time. If you can find someone better for the job, replace me."

If the candidate points out the consequences of continued poor performance, say:

5.	"I know, but it does not make this job any more bearable."

If the candidate points out your attitude is inappropriate/unacceptable or outlines you could be reported for under performance, say:

6.	"Yeah, and what you going to do next, move me to a punishment posting? Oh, I forgot, I'm already in the worst job in the force."

If the candidate asks why you think custody sergeant is the worst/most unpopular role, say.

7.	"It's always busy and you never get a break."

If the candidate points out the importance of having a break or suggests ways of doing so, say.

8.	"Yeah, I've heard it all before, it never gets done for real."

If the candidate asks what the other custody sergeants are feeling/thinking, say.

9.	"I think everyone is tired and fed up."

If the candidate asks if there was something significant about the 17th and 18th of last month, say:

10.	"I was really tired; there has been a lot of cancelled days off and long shifts without a break."

If the candidate asks about the lack of breaks or cancelled days off and long shifts, say.

11. **"Too many people are off sick and the rest of us are having to work more."**

   If the candidate asks what your career aspirations are or for your views on your role as custody sergeant, say.

12. **"Custody is not what I want to do. I'm wasting all my specialist skills. I want to be a uniform patrol sergeant or return as a sergeant to a specialist road policing role."**

   If the candidate points out how your skills can be of benefit/use in the custody sergeant role, say.

13. **"Yeah, but it's still not what I want to do with my life."**

   If the candidate points out the importance of the role of custody sergeant, say.

14. **"Right and that's why it's such a popular role."**

Role actor instructions debrief

After reading through the role actor instructions you will be aware of the issues surrounding Alston. Imagine that you are in your room at the assessment centre and the buzzer indicating that the role actor and assessor are entering the room has just sounded.

The role actor enters the room and delivers role actor response 1, as outlined in the role actor script. The role actor confirms their identity to you and that the chief inspector has informed them to come and see you.

You should immediately refer to Inspector Kerr's memorandum. Remember, the order in which you use the candidate information for an exercise makes no difference to how you are assessed.

Ask Alston about the incident relating to Morrison and you will receive role actor response 2. How would you react to that response? There are clearly two issues to address but we will wait until we debrief the assessment checklist to cover those points.

You should then ask Alston about the bail conditions imposed on Gold which would prompt role actor response 3. How would you react to this response?

At this point you should outline to Alston the consequences of their decision in relation to one or both of the incidents and receive role actor response 4. How would you react to this response? By now you should have realised that all is not well with Alston and the role they are performing, and it is clear you need to address their attitude. Remember to do this within the bounds of Respect for Race and Diversity.

Role actor response 5 could follow on almost immediately, particularly if you outline the consequences of continuing with their current attitude or performance.

By addressing their attitude you would receive role actor response 6. It is patently clear by now that Alston does not want to perform the custody sergeant role.

By listening to the role actor you would pick up on the fact that Alston mentioned it was the 'worse job in the force', so you seek to clarify why that is the case. Role actor response 7 provides you with information that you can address. You are the divisional Inspector and should consider the welfare of all of your staff.

You suggest options to assist the custody sergeants and receive role actor response 8.

As the divisional Inspector you want to know if Alston's opinions are shared by the other custody sergeants. You check this out with Alston and receive role actor response 9. It is now clear that you need to do something about the current situation. You are the link with the divisional senior management team and can take forward Alston's concerns.

That was a brief synopsis of how an interaction between you and the role actor could take place. Always be prepared to react to the role actor but do not forget also to refer to your candidate information.

Did you identify when reading through the incidents outlined in Inspector Kerr's memorandum that the incidents were on consecutive days, 17th and 18th? Remember it is important to concentrate during that preparatory phase at the assessment centre and ensure you read all of the candidate information. I purposely included the dates in the exercise to reinforce this point. Role actor response 10 explains why Alston acted as they did on the dates mentioned.

To add weight to Alston's argument, if you review the candidate information you will see that there were no performance issues before or after these two days.

Role actor response 11 suggests that you need to treat the custody office staffing as a priority.

Following role actor response 4 you may have asked Alston what their career ambitions were. Role actor response 12 would have resulted.

Role actor response 13 is another indication that Alston does not want to carry on with the custody sergeant role.

Role actor response 14 should indicate to you that the post should be made more attractive to others. Perhaps addressing the resourcing issues may help to do this.

Assessment checklist

Competency Area	Scalar	Grade
Area 1: Maximising Potential **Outlines:** 1.1 role actor's previous good performance 1.2 the importance custody sergeant role 1.3 Offers support for role actor's future career aspirations	Clear – Unclear 1 2 3 4 5	A B C D
Area 2: Problem Solving **Asks role actor:** 2.1 about their career aspirations 2.2 why custody such an unpopular role 2.3 why lack of rest days/breaks, and such long hours. 2.4 Identifies that mistakes were on consecutive days	Thorough – Superficial	
Area 3: Planning and Organising **Outlines options:** 3.1 for taking breaks 3.2 for improving staffing levels in custody 3.3 making custody role more popular to others	Thorough – Superficial 1 2 3 4 5	A B C D
Area 4: Strategic Perspective: **Informs role actor:** 4.1 should not keep a cell free just in case 4.2 continued poor performance unacceptable 4.3 custody staffing situation unacceptable **Explains consequences:** 4.4 of poor performance to investigations 4.5 of poor performance to role actor's career	Thorough – Superficial 1 2 3 4 5	A B C D
Area 5: Respect for Race and Diversity	Sensitive – Insensitive 1 2 3 4 5 Objective – Biased 1 2 3 4 5	A B C D

Assessment checklist debrief

The Alston exercise contains five competency areas; Maximising Potential, Problem Solving, Planning and Organising, Strategic Perspective and Respect for Race and Diversity. No one competency area carries more weight or importance than another in the assessment process.

The exercise contains 15 behavioural statements (statements a candidate should say). Remember, there will be no more than six and no less than three behavioural statements in a competency area. Respect for Race and Diversity does not contain behavioural statements.

We will now take each competency area and behavioural statement in turn. Have your candidate information and role actor notes to hand to see which behavioural statements you would have scored.

Area 1: Maximising Potential
This area contains three behavioural statements. Notice that 1.1 and 1.2 are prefixed by 'Outlines'. The scalar (how well a candidate scores the behavioural statements) for this area is Clear to Unclear.

1.1 ... role actor's previous good performance. Although the candidate information outlines a number of performance issues and Alston's attitude requires addressing, the candidate information does contain positive aspects of Alston's performance in the chief inspector's memorandum.

1.2 ... the importance of custody sergeant role. You could outline the importance of the role to reassure Alston that their work plays a key part in the organisation.

1.3 Offers support for role actor's future career aspirations. Alston indicates that they do want to move on. As their supervisor you should offer your support for their future career development.

Area 2: Problem Solving
This area contains four behavioural statements. Notice that 2.1, 2.2 and 2.3 are prefixed by 'Asks role actor'. The scalar for this area is Thorough to Superficial.

2.1 ... about their career aspirations. Asking what Alston wants from their career would result in role actor response 12. Behavioural statement 1.3 could be scored immediately following 2.1. You do not have to systematically work your way down an assessment checklist. If you say something that constitutes an assessment checklist behavioural statement at anytime during the five-minute interaction you will score it.

2.2 ... why custody such an unpopular role. As the divisional inspector you need to clarify why this is the case. Role actor response 7 would provide you with the answer.

2.3 ... why lack of rest days/breaks, and such long hours. This question would be asked following the information contained in role actor response 10. Role actor response 11 would provide you with the details.

2.4 Identifies that mistakes were on consecutive days. Perhaps this is the key to the exercise. I mentioned in the role actor instructions debrief that it is important to read all of the candidate information. Identifying the consecutive days would prompt role actor response 10. As you will see, that opens up the opportunity to score behavioural statements 3.1 and 3.2 on the assessment checklist.

Area 3: Planning and Organising
This area contains the minimum three behavioural statements. Notice that all are prefixed by 'Outlines options'. The scalar for this area is Thorough to Superficial.

3.1 ... for taking breaks. This would be your response to role actor response 7 or 10. Perhaps suggesting support from divisional sergeants would address this problem.

3.2 ... for improving staffing levels in custody. The support of divisional sergeants or constables could also be suggested here. Perhaps the staffing structure of the custody office requires reviewing. You are the divisional Inspector and should now be considering these issues.

3.3 ... making custody role more popular to others. To address the staffing problem more staff may be required. In order to achieve this the role needs to appeal to others. Ensuring assistance from divisional staff may go someway towards doing this. Once this is in place, attachments could be offered to potential applicants in order for them to gain an appreciation of the role. These are only examples, no doubt you will have thought of your own options.

Area 4: Strategic Perspective
This area contains five behavioural statements. Notice that 4.1, 4.2 and

4.3 are prefixed by 'Informs role actor'. Behavioural statements 4.3 and 4.4 are prefixed by 'Explains consequences'. The scalar for this area is Thorough to Superficial.

4.1 ... should not keep a cell free just in case. This should be pointed to Alston following the delivery of role actor response 2. If you followed Alston's reasoning there would always be a free cell!

4.2 ... continued poor performance unacceptable. This certainly needs to be addressed with Alston and pointed out. This is one behavioural statement that displays why it is essential to get into the role of an Inspector. Role actor response 5 would follow.

4.3 ... custody staffing situation is unacceptable. As the divisional Inspector you need to acknowledge this, particularly in light of the information in role actor response 11. The current situation cannot be allowed to continue as it is having an affect on individual officers' health and performance.

4.4 ... of poor performance to investigations. You would have no doubt identified the consequences of Alston's actions in the two incidents outlined in Inspector Kerr's memorandum. Mentioning loss of evidence, impeding the investigation, impression given to other officers, offenders escaping justice and image of police would be the type of comments that would score this behavioural statement.

4.5 ... of poor performance to role actor's career. There is also the effect on Alston personally. At some point they may want to move on, yet performing in such a manner could delay or prevent such a move. Their previously good reputation could also be affected.

Area 5: Respect for Race and Diversity
This competency area does not contain behavioural statements. You are assessed across the five-minute interaction against two scalars, in this case Sensitive to Insensitive and Objective to Biased.

You need to be sensitive to Alston's needs and the reason why they have performed in the manner described. I know this may be difficult when confronted with a role actor of Alston's demeanour but it is essential to maintain a balanced view when dealing with the exercises. This is relevant to both police and non-police exercises.

Candidate instructions

In this exercise you will receive three pages of preparatory information:

- a memorandum from Chief Inspector Venerdi
- a letter from the Crown Prosecution Service (CPS)
- a memorandum from Sergeant J Emerson

During the activity phase you will meet Sergeant J Emerson.

CASTLESHIRE POLICE

Memorandum

From: Chief Inspector Venerdi, Castleside

To: Inspector 'Candidate', Castleside

Subject: Defendant John Crow

Date: yesterday

Attached is a letter from the Crown Prosecution Services (CPS), the contents of which give me some concern.

Constable Huntley was the officer responsible for this investigation. He is nearing the end of his probation. Early in his probationary period he had good reports from his tutor constable. The officer has recently transferred to team 3 where his supervisor is Sergeant Emerson.

Sergeant Emerson was asked by your predecessor to investigate the matter outlined and I have attached a copy of the sergeant's response. The response is insufficient to submit to the CPS. As time is pressing on it is now even more urgent that this matter is dealt with fully so I have arranged for Sergeant Emerson to speak to you on your first day.

L Venerdi

Chief Inspector Venerdi

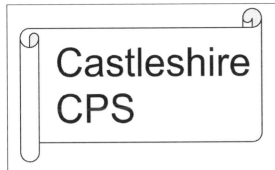

Castleshire CPS

Dear Chief Inspector Venerdi,   Date: one week ago

Case regarding defendant John Crow

I feel I have to draw the above case to your attention in view of the substantial delay in our request sent two weeks ago for an update regarding the absence of a key statement.

Crow was charged with an offence of Section 20 Grievous Bodily Harm that took place 11 months ago. The evidence for this case was straightforward and some 9 months ago the officer was advised that medical evidence was required to be able to ascertain the level of assault charge. At this point the victim had been referred to Castleshire County Hospital but no evidence had been obtained to show that his jaw was broken and required an operation to fix plates in order to heal the fracture.

It is unclear what happened, although there is a statement that was obtained from the oral surgeon last month. On the MG6 and MG6A it simply says that there was a long wait for the medical statement but does not explain why.

In view of the nature of the charge, this is a matter that is likely to end up at crown court before a judge who, no doubt, will require a full explanation as to the delay in these proceedings. I would therefore ask that you look into this particular matter.

Many thanks for your kind assistance in this matter.

Yours sincerely

Ali Penifer

A J Penifer

CASTLESHIRE POLICE

Memorandum

From:	Sergeant Emerson, team 3, Castleside
To:	Chief Inspector Venerdi, Castleside
Subject:	Constable Huntley
Date:	yesterday

In response to the letter from the CPS regarding the defendant John Crow, I have to report that the officer had to frequently re-bail this defendant because of failure by the local hospital to provide a statement from the specialist surgeon. I have been assured by Constable Huntley that he has made numerous attempts to obtain this statement.

For your information Constable Huntley is an enthusiastic member of the team, frequently volunteering to attend incidents. He is hard working, is always keen, and is flexible and willing to change shifts at short notice.

J Emerson

Sergeant Emerson

Candidate information debrief

Have you started to put yourself under the time constraints of the actual Part II assessment centre yet when reading through the candidate information? Remember in total you have 45 minutes preparation time. After 43 minutes the assessment centre buzzer will sound to warn you that in two minutes the first role actor and assessor will enter the room. This two minute warning will give you an opportunity to turn back to the first exercise in your book and refresh your memory with its contents. This equates to six minutes preparation time per exercise. However, do not worry if you exceed this amount of time. Some exercises may contain more candidate information that another. The exercise design process ensures that overall you should have sufficient time.

How did you get on with the Emerson exercise candidate information? How did you feel when you read on the exercise front cover that you had three pages of information to read? Two of the documents do not require a lot of reading, in fact, the lack of content in Emerson's memorandum is one of the issues contained in the exercise.

Memorandum from Chief Inspector Venerdi
The opening line of the chief inspector's memorandum perhaps gives an indication of what is to come. If it causes the Chief Inspector some concern then it should cause you concern too. After all you are Emerson's supervisor.

The second paragraph provides you with information regarding Constable Huntley, a member of Emerson's team. The officer is nearing the end of his probationary period and has recently transferred to team 3. Did you consider this information to be significant? Do you feel you want to enquire as to why Huntley has recently transferred to team 3?

The next paragraph informs you that Emerson was given a CPS enquiry by your predecessor and has only just responded. The chief inspector clearly states that the response is insufficient to submit to the CPS and emphasises that the matter is now urgent. This should indicate to you that you need to address the matter forthwith and give clear direction to Emerson as to how the matter should progress.

Letter from A Penifer, CPS
You should have noticed that the letter is dated one week ago. The first paragraph emphasises the importance and urgency of the enquiry and

informs you of the reason for the letter being sent; that a file has been submitted minus a key statement.

The next paragraph provides you with details of the case in question. Alarmingly, the offence occurred 11 months previous. A statement has been received from Castleshire County Hospital outlining details of the victim's injuries.

A statement was finally obtained last month but there is no indication on the case papers as to why there was a substantial delay.

A full explanation as to the delay is required because the case is to be heard at crown court.

This letter should have raised issues for you. For example, why was there no response to the request sent two weeks ago? Why did it take so long to obtain the statement? When did Emerson take supervisory responsibility for Constable Huntley?

Memorandum from Sergeant Emerson

As I have already mentioned, the lack of detail in this memorandum is one of the issues in this exercise.

It is another document that raises more questions for you. In particular, what action had Constable Huntley taken to obtain the statement? The memorandum states he made numerous attempts. How many?

Did you make a note to pursue the comment in the statement that Emerson 'has been assured by Constable Huntley that he has made numerous attempts to obtain the statement'? What does this comment suggest to you? Did you consider that Emerson might not be monitoring Constable Huntley's work as thoroughly as they should? These are questions you should consider putting to Emerson.

The memorandum outlines that Constable Huntley is an enthusiastic, hard working team member. This supports the information in Chief Inspector Venerdi's memorandum that Huntley performs to a high standard. This information would seem to eliminate the possibility that the statement was not obtained because of Constable Huntley's attitude or lack of commitment.

Role actor instructions

You are Sergeant Joe/Jo Emerson and you have five years' service, all of which have been on uniform patrol duties. You were promoted six months ago from the neighbouring Mayford Division to Castleside where you are the team 3 Sergeant. You have never received any supervisor/management training or conducted any acting duties.

You know Constable Huntley is happily married and are not aware of the officer having any personal issues or problems. Constable Huntley moved to your team three months ago, as it was a better match to his wife's work. You have read the officers previous reports, which show him to be keen and enthusiastic.

You did not receive a handover from the previous team 3 sergeant and have been left to get on with your role by the inspector. You have concentrated on making sure all incidents are attended and dealt with properly, but have taken little notice of ongoing investigations. You ask staff about their workload and expect your officers to raise any problems they may have. None have come to you with anything more than straightforward questions, which you were able to deal with.

You have spoken to Constable Huntley concerning the case of John Crow and had been vaguely aware that he had been awaiting medical evidence. Knowing Constable Huntley to be hard working, you had not challenged him or asked for any specific details. You have not made any enquiries regarding the case with Constable Huntley's previous supervisor.

You will be appreciative of any assistance offered.

Demeanour: confident.

When you enter the room, say:

1. **"Hello Inspector I'm Sergeant Joe/Jo Emerson. Chief Inspector Venerdi requested I see you about Constable Huntley."**

   If the candidate asks about your relationship with/opinion of Constable Huntley, say:

2. **"He's a good member of the team and, other than this small matter, is working well."**

   If the candidate asks you about the case concerning Crow, say:

3. "He brought the investigation with him, I only know he was having difficulties getting a doctor's statement from the hospital."

   If the candidate asks about the difficulties obtaining the doctor's statement, say:

4. "I think he followed the procedure and sent a request to the hospital and I think he phoned them and called in several times."

   If the candidate asks when the requests were made for the statement from the hospital, say:

5. "I think it has been going on since the offence but I do not know the exact dates."

   If the candidate asks what guidance/supervision you gave Huntley, say:

6. "Well I asked him how his work was going and just told him to keep trying, these things can take time."

   If the candidate asks about other team member's investigations, say:

7. "All the officers say they only have recent crime investigations."

   If the candidate points out you did not give sufficient guidance/should conduct checks file progress, say:

8. "I was trying to do my best."

   If the candidate asks what training/guidance you have had, say:

9. "Nothing really, I've just tried to get on with it."

   If the candidate points out the report/investigation for the chief inspector did not contain sufficient detail/you should submit a more detailed report, say:

10. "I hadn't realised I needed to give more information."

    If the candidate suggests options as to what you should do in the future, say:

11. "I understand now, I'll certainly do that next time."

Role actor instructions debrief

As you can see from the role actor instructions, Emerson has five years' service. They were only promoted into their current post six months ago. To compound their inexperience in the role they have not received any training for the role or previously performed acting sergeant duties. Of course, when you meet the role actor you will be unaware of these facts and will have to draw this information from them by asking the relevant questions.

Emerson is not aware of any personal problems being experienced by Constable Huntley. Huntley transferred to team 3 for personal reasons. This eliminates any performance issues you might have suspected caused Huntley to transfer to team 3.

Emerson has not received any handover from the previous team 3 sergeant and your predecessor has just left Emerson to get on with their role. Emerson has not been monitoring team 3 members' investigations or workload.

Emerson is aware of the case of John Crow and is vaguely aware that he had been awaiting medical evidence. However, Emerson did not challenge Huntley or ask for details of the case. Emerson has not made any enquiries with Huntley's previous supervisor regarding the Crow case.

When you read the role actor instructions background did you consider that the exercise issues had changed from those you identified as being contained in the candidate information?

The opening response of the role actor instructions confirms the role actor's identity and that your meeting concerns Constable Huntley.

Role actor response 2 confirms that Huntley is a good team member and is generally performing to the required standard. Remember, at this point you are still unaware of Emerson's inexperience in their role.

Role actor response 3 provides you with the information that Huntley brought the investigation with them when they transferred to team 3. However, this response does not inform you how long Emerson has been responsible for Huntley's supervision. Ascertaining that information would give you an indication of how long Emerson has been aware of the problem with the Crow case.

Role actor response 4 should raise some concerns for you. The response is very vague and does not contain any accurate information as to the enquiries Huntley has made with the hospital. It appears to be very much guesswork on Emerson's part. This should cause you some concern.

Role actor response 5 is equally as vague about the hospital enquiries. By now you should be concerned at the vagueness of Emerson's responses to your questions concerning the statement.

Role actor response 6 gives you an indication, perhaps, that Emerson is not monitoring the enquiry or providing Huntley with the correct amount of guidance. Again this should cause you some concern.

Role actor response 7 also suggests that Emerson is not fully carrying out their supervisory duties. It would appear they are relying on individual officer's honesty to monitor the team's ongoing investigations.

Role actor response 8 provides an indication that Emerson is not fully confident or competent in their role. It would, therefore, be quite natural to follow up this response with asking what training or preparation they have had for their role. Role actor response 9 would be the result. This information would provide you with the reason why Emerson is not confident or competent in the role.

The concerns raised in the CPS letter have still not been addressed, so you must inform Emerson of this fact. Role actor response 10 would then be delivered. Perhaps this response also indicates that Emerson is not confident or competent in their role.

Role actor response 11 provides you with reassurance that Emerson will perform more competently in the future.

I'm sure that the information from the role actor would certainly have altered your view of the exercise and the reasons why you considered events were occurring. No doubt you now appreciate why it is important you keep an open mind when reading through your candidate information and why it is important to use the role actor as your other source of information.

Assessment checklist

Competency Area	Scalar	Grade
Area 1: Maximising Potential	Clear – Unclear 1 2 3 4 5	A B C D
1.1 Explains role actor has responsibility to monitor officer's files/investigations 1.2 Offers role actor training/development 1.3 Explains Huntley's enthusiasm may be affecting his investigations 1.4 Outlines importance of monitoring Huntley's performance		
Area 2: Effective Communication **Outlines role actor should:**	Thorough – Superficial 1 2 3 4 5	A B C D
2.1 monitor Huntley's work 2.2 conduct more thorough investigation 2.3 resubmit more detailed report 2.4 Outlines importance of expeditious investigation of offences		
Area 3: Problem Solving **Asks role actor:**	Thorough – Superficial 1 2 3 4 5	A B C D
3.1 what advice/assistance given to Huntley 3.2 about their supervisory experience/ training 3.3 why Huntley transferred to team 3 3.4 how long Huntley been on team 3 3.5 if any other historic outstanding investigations on team		
Area 4: Respect for Race and Diversity	Sensitive – Insensitive 1 2 3 4 5 Supportive – Unsupportive 1 2 3 4 5	A B C D

Assessment checklist debrief

The Emerson exercise contains four competency areas; Maximising Potential, Effective Communication, Problem Solving, and Respect for Race and Diversity.

The exercise contains 13 behavioural statements (statements a candidate should say). Remember, there will be no more than six and no less than three behavioural statements in a competency area. Respect for Race and Diversity does not contain behavioural statements.

We will now take each competency area and behavioural statement in turn. Have your candidate information and role actor notes to hand to see which behavioural statements you would have scored.

Area 1: Maximising Potential

This area contains four behavioural statements. The scalar (how well a candidate scores the behavioural statements) for this area is Clear to Unclear.

1.1 Explains role actor has responsibility to monitor officer's files/investigations. Emerson is the team 3 Sergeant and must take on their responsibilities to the team. It is clear from the role actor responses 6 and 7 that this is not the case at present. As their supervisor, you should instruct them to do so. This behavioural statement is an example of why you must take on the role of an inspector.

1.2 Offers role actor training/development. As a supervisor you have a responsibility to develop your staff. Emerson has not had any training or development to prepare them for their role. You should rectify this as soon as possible.

1.3 Explains Huntley's enthusiasm may be affecting his investigations. There is an indication that this may be the case by the information in Emerson's memorandum. Huntley frequently volunteers to attend incidents and is willing to change shifts at short notice. Consequently they may be neglecting their outstanding investigations.

1.4 Outlines importance of monitoring Huntley's performance. Huntley is still in the probationary period. Consequently they require monitoring and support, as they are inexperienced. Monitoring their work may prevent a reoccurrence of the problems experienced in the Crow case.

Area 2: Effective Communication

This area contains four behavioural statements. Notice that 2.1, 2.2 and 2.3 are prefixed by 'Outlines role actor should'. The scalar for this area is Thorough to Superficial.

Behavioural statements 2.1, 2.2 and 2.3 relate to you taking on the role of the inspector and providing direction to one of the sergeants for whom you have responsibility. Should you not do this in this exercise you would fail to score three out of four behavioural statements in one competency area. This would have a very detrimental affect on your overall grade for this competency area.

2.1 ... monitor Huntley's work. This behavioural statement provides clear direction to Emerson as to what is required in future regarding Huntley. Behavioural statement 1.4 could be scored immediately after by outlining why Huntley should be monitored.

2.2 ... conduct more thorough investigation. The CPS enquiry has not been answered. Emerson is responsible for the enquiry and should be directed to complete it.

2.3 ... re-submit more detailed report. Once the enquiry is complete Emerson should be informed that a more detailed report needs to be submitted.

2.4 Outlines importance of expeditious investigation of offences. Outlining the fact that cases could be lost at court, that no evidence may have to be offered or the effect on how the police are perceived would, be the type of comments that would score this behavioural statement.

Area 3: Problem Solving

This area contains five behavioural statements. Notice that all are prefixed by 'Asks role actor'. The scalar for this area is Thorough to Superficial.

3.1 ... what advice/assistance given to Huntley. Huntley is a probationer constable. Perhaps he is unsure how to progress in the Crow case or lacked confidence in pressing the hospital for the statement. Did Emerson assist Huntley? Role actor response 6 would be the result of asking this question.

3.2 ... about their supervisory experience/training. This question is key to the exercise. The role actor would provide role actor response 9.

3.3 ... why Huntley transferred to team 3. You may feel that you need to know this information to inform you of any performance issues with Huntley.

3.4 ... how long Huntley has been on team 3. The Crow case has been ongoing for 11 months. Chief Inspector Venerdi's memorandum states that Huntley transferred to team 3 recently. So how long has Emerson had supervisory responsibility for Huntley?

3.5 ... if any other historic outstanding investigations on team. You may feel when talking to Emerson that the problem with outstanding investigations is not just confined to Huntley and the Crow case. Role actor response 7 would suggest this may be the case. Asking this question would assist in establishing just how widespread the problem is.

Area 4: Respect for Race and Diversity

This competency area does not contain behavioural statements. You are assessed across the five-minute interaction against two scalars, in this case Sensitive to Insensitive and Supportive to Unsupportive.

Emerson is unprepared and untrained to take on the sergeant role. You need to be sensitive to this and offer the officer your support. However, you must also address their performance issues in a sensitive and supportive manner.

Candidate instructions

In this exercise you will receive two pages of preparatory information:

- a memorandum from Chief Inspector Venerdi
- a copy of an article from the Castleside Echo

During the activity phase you will meet Sergeant A Heal.

CASTLESHIRE POLICE

Memorandum

From:	Chief Inspector Venerdi, Castleside
To:	Inspector 'Candidate', Castleside
Subject:	Sergeant A Heal
Date:	yesterday

I have been made aware by a member of our police staff of a conversation in the canteen recently where Sergeant Heal was overheard to say to a colleague: "With the Community Support Officers you get what you pay for, and if you pay peanuts, what do you expect?"

In addition to this, I have just read the attached article in last week's Castleside Echo, which causes me obvious concern. The report referred to in the article was an internal report.

Sergeant Heal transferred to Castleside three months ago and took on the role as supervisor for the team of 12 CSOs. The officer has 15 years' service and has been a sergeant for two years. They came to the district with an excellent reputation having a background as a constable in CID and on promotion, turned around a poorly performing team at Northside.

I would have liked to have dealt with these matters myself, but as I am away for two weeks and you will have supervisory responsibility for Sergeant Heal, I thought it would be more appropriate for you to deal with this. I have arranged for Sergeant Heal to see you on your first day.

L Venerdi

Chief Inspector

CASTLESIDE ECHO – LAST WEEK'S EDITION

MISTRUST RUINS RELATIONS BETWEEN POLICE AND CSO 'SCARECROWS'

Lynn York reports

The relationship between Community Support Officers and regular officers has been further brought into question following the publication of a leaked report that labels CSOs as 'mobile scarecrows'. Relations with sworn-in police officers are all too often marked by 'competition and mistrust'.

It is suggested that there are some urgent problems with the CSOs. These include the fact that they are poorly organised and relationships with full-time officers vary considerably from co-operation to mutual indifference and rivalry.

The report suggests there is 'a degree of confusion' among CSOs who, it states, are sometimes unsure what to do beyond walking their beat.

We spoke to members of the community, who have stated they have found it 'off-putting' to see CSOs apparently 'more concerned with their personal conversations' than the job in hand, thereby sending out a message of 'we do not wish to be disturbed'.

CSOs receive only five weeks training, including two weeks on the beat. Another concern is that in giving CSOs increased powers, they are likely to be drawn into even more dangerous situations.

No one was available for comment at Castleside Police at the time of going to press.

Candidate information debrief

How did you cope with the candidate information for the Heal exercise? Did you put yourself under the time constraints of the assessment centre as I suggested in the previous exercise?

Memorandum from Chief Inspector Venerdi

The first paragraph of the memorandum immediately outlines to you one of the exercise issues: the comment made by Sergeant Heal in the staff canteen. What were your thoughts when you read the comment Heal made in relation to the Community Support Officers? The comment was made to a member of police staff by a police officer in a supervisory role. Did you make a note of what the consequences of that comment could be, not only to Heal but to the organisation? When reading through the exercise candidate information, you should always consider the consequences of a person's actions or lack of action.

To compound Heal's comments regarding the CSOs, an article has appeared in the local press that speaks of CSOs in less than favourable terms. Is the publication of the article taking place at the same time as Heal's comment an unhappy coincidence or are the two incidents connected? Did you consider the two might be linked? Even more alarming is the fact that the content of the newspaper article came from a leaked internal report. What did you consider in relation to this piece of information?

The memorandum then provides you with background to Heal's experience. It should have caused you concern when you discovered that Heal is the CSO team supervisor, having taken on the role three months ago. So why is Heal making disparaging comments about their own team? Heal is an experienced officer and has been a sergeant for two years. This fact should rule out any indication that there is a training requirement to address Heal's supervisory skills. This is compounded with the information that they were promoted out of the CID and subsequently, as a sergeant, addressed the inadequate performance of a team in another division.

The final paragraph of the memorandum clearly informs you that you have supervisory responsibility for Heal and therefore you are to deal with the matters outlined in the memorandum.

A point worth noting is that the memorandum does not tell you to resolve the matter. That would be unfair to you and unrealistic. If this were a matter that were to require your attention in your current day-to-day role, you would obviously take longer than five minutes to deal with it. Consequently, you will not be expected to resolve issues within the five-minute interaction. You would however be expected to display your potential to perform the rank of inspector by dealing with the issues contained within the exercise.

Castleside Echo article

Although the article sounds sensationalist, it does contain comments that should cause you concern. The opening paragraph refers to the CSOs as 'mobile scarecrows' and intimates that relations with police officers is tainted by 'competition and mistrust'. If this situation does exist then it needs to be addressed.

The article continues, stating that the CSOs are poorly organised and their relationship with police officers is unstable. Has Heal had experience of this?

The CSOs' understanding of their role is then brought into question in the third paragraph.

The next paragraph, which outlines the views of the community, is equally alarming to you as the divisional Inspector. Did you consider how widespread these views might be held in the community? Did you consider how the perception of CSOs by the community might be addressed?

The article then provides you with details of the CSO training.

Finally the article informs you that no one from Castleshire Police was available for comment. What did you consider in relation to this piece of information?

From the candidate information, you should have identified a number of issues or comments you wish to clarify in your meeting with Heal.

Role actor instructions

You are Andrew/Andrea Heal. You are married and have fifteen years' service. You spent five years on the CID before being promoted to Northside two years ago. You established yourself as an operational sergeant and earned a very good reputation, having turned around team 2 from the worst to the best performing team on the district. You did this by utilising your CID experience and creating a positive team spirit.

Three months ago you transferred to Castleside and took on the role of supervisory sergeant for the 12 CSOs. You took on the role, as you believed it would widen your experience. You have recently become disillusioned, as you feel constrained by the limited powers that the CSOs have and wish you were back with your team at Northside. You saw very little of the previous Inspector.

Last week you were in the canteen with a colleague when you said, 'With the CSOs you get what you pay for and if you pay peanuts, what do you expect?' At the time you felt frustrated because you wanted to run an operation but didn't bother as your team of CSOs have limited powers. Overall, you get on well with the individuals on your team.

You have seen the article in the Castleside Echo and, whilst in agreement with some of the issues, you are concerned about the effect it may have on your team. You do not know who leaked the report to the press.

Demeanour: confident

When you enter the room, say:

1. **"Hello inspector I'm Andrew/Andrea Heal. Chief Inspector Venerdi left me a note to come and see you."**

    If the candidate asks how you feel about your current role, say:

2. **"It's alright but it's a bit restrictive at times as the CSOs don't have the powers the regulars do."**

    If the candidate asks how you are getting on with the CSOs on your team, say:

3. **"Overall fine. They're a good group of people but it's not the same as running a team of regulars."**

    If the candidate asks if you made the comment about the CSOs in the canteen, say:

4. "Yes. The fact is this: they are not regular officers and it's policing on the cheap."

If the candidate points out that your attitude is unacceptable, say:

5. "I hear what you are saying. I just want to get on with the job."

If the candidate points out the potential consequences of the comment, say:

6. "I understand what you are saying. I hadn't thought about it like that."

If the candidate asks why you transferred to Castleside/took on CSO supervisor role, say:

7. "I thought by transferring and taking on this role, it would widen my experience. I feel like giving this job up."

If the candidate asks if you have seen the article in the *Castleside Echo*, say:

8. "I read it when it came out. I can see where they're coming from."

If the candidate asks if you have discussed the article with your team/if they have made comment themselves, say:

9. "I haven't discussed it with them. I thought it better just to keep quiet."

If the candidate suggests contacting the *Castleside Echo* to give the police response, say:

10. "If you think that will help. I hadn't considered that."

If the candidate suggests arranging a meeting with the CSO team to reassure them, say:

11. "I'll do that. They would probably appreciate it. I understand what you are saying.

If the candidate acknowledges your previous experiences/future support, say:

12. "Thanks Inspector. I appreciate that. I want to make the most of the opportunity."

Role actor instructions debrief

The opening paragraph outlines details of Heal's police service and the fact that they turned around an under performing team at Northside.

Heal transferred to Castleside three months ago to take on the role of CSO team supervisor. The team comprises of 12 CSOs. Heal believed this would widen his/her supervisory experience. However, Heal has recently become frustrated with the role of CSO team supervisor, as they feel constrained by the limited powers that CSOs have. They feel that they no longer want to continue in this role. They had little contact with the previous inspector, your predecessor. In light of this information, how do you now view Heal's attitude towards the CSOs?

The role actor instructions then continue by outlining the comment Heal made in the canteen regarding the CSOs. It also provides a reason why Heal made the comment.

The final paragraph outlines that Heal does not know who leaked the report to the press. Of course you will have to ask Heal to get this information.

The opening role actor response confirms the role actor's identity and the fact that Chief Inspector Venerdi has asked Heal to come and see you. Obviously, at this point Heal is unaware what the meeting concerns.

Role actor response 2 provides you with an indication that Heal is not totally satisfied with their role. You may feel that you want to clarify why Heal considers the role to be restrictive. If so you would receive the information in the role actor instructions relating to the operation Heal wanted to run.

Role actor response 3 also suggests that Heal is dissatisfied with their role but appears to have a good relationship with their team.

The question contained in the prompt for role actor response 4 could quite conceivably be asked at the very start of the five-minute interaction. Heal does not deny saying the comment and compounds their views by further stating 'it's policing on the cheap'. How would you respond to this comment?

Hopefully by pointing out that Heals comments and/or attitude regarding CSOs is unacceptable, particularly as they are the team supervisor. Doing this would result in you receiving role actor response 5.

It may be pertinent at this point to outline to you that a role actor never tells lies nor it is part of their role to deliberately mislead you. For example, Heal would not deny making the comment in the canteen. That would be unfair to you and would disadvantage the way you deal with the exercise.

Role actor response 6 is delivered as a result of you outlining the consequences of the comment. This could be to Heal personally, to the organisation or to the CSOs.

Role actor response 7 provides you with the reason why Heal took on the CSO supervisor role. However, it also indicates that Heal now feels like leaving the role. Heal has only performed the role for three months. They have shown they can lead a team by their performance at Northside. Surely it would better if they remained in post?

You could receive role actor response 8 early in the interaction if you want to confirm whether or not Heal has any involvement in the newspaper article. Further questioning would confirm they were not involved in the article or in its leaking to the press.

Role actor response 9 informs you that Heal has not discussed the article with the CSOs. If you received this reply what would you consider doing in your role as the divisional Inspector?

Role actor response 10 follows your suggestion of contacting the Castleside Echo.

Role actor response 11 also follows a suggestion on your part to address the CSOs. I will cover the prompts to role actor responses 10 and 11 when we debrief the exercise assessment checklist.

Role actor response 12 would follow your suggestion that Heal remains in their current role as you feel they have a lot to offer. It is possible that this suggestion by you could follow role actor response 7.

Assessment checklist

Competency Area	Scalar	Grade
Area 1: Effective Communication **Asks role actor:** 1.1 if made comment in canteen 1.2 if made comments to/aware of who informed Castleside Echo 1.3 why transferred to Castleside 1.4 Suggests role actor contacts Castleside Echo to respond to article	Thorough – Superficial 1 2 3 4 5	A B C D
Area 2: Maximising Potential **Acknowledges:** 2.1 role actor's past performance/experience 2.2 role as supervisor/role model. 2.3 Asks role actor for views on role as CSO supervisor 2.4 Encourages role actor to continue in role	Thorough – Superficial 1 2 3 4 5	A B C D
Area 3: Personal Responsibility **Informs role actor:** 3.1 that comments in canteen are unacceptable 3.2 will speak to CSO Team 3.3 will monitor future conduct/comments 3.4 will investigate leaked report to press **Outlines consequences:** 3.5 of making comments in canteen (e.g. perception/code of conduct/affect on CSOs) 3.6 of newspaper article	Clear – Unclear 1 2 3 4 5	A B C D
Area 4: Respect for Race and Diversity	Objective – Biased 1 2 3 4 5 Supportive – Unsupportive 1 2 3 4 5	A B C D

Assessment checklist debrief

The Heal exercise contains four competency areas; Effective Communication, Maximising Potential, Personal Responsibility and Respect for Race and Diversity.

The exercise contains 14 behavioural statements (statements a candidate should say). Remember there will be no more than six and no less than three behavioural statements in a competency area. Respect for Race and Diversity does not contain behavioural statements.

We will now take each competency area and behavioural statement in turn. Have your candidate information and role actor notes to hand to see which behavioural statements you would have scored.

Area 1: Effective Communication

This area contains four behavioural statements. Notice that 1.1, 1.2 and 1.3 are prefixed by 'Asks role actor'. The scalar (how well a candidate scores the behavioural statements) for this area is Thorough to Superficial.

1.1 ... if made comment in canteen. Clarifying Heal made the comment would result in role actor response 4. Asking why they made the comment may result in a higher scalar for this behavioural statement. Remember there is always a reason why someone has acted in the way described in the candidate information.

1.2 ... if made comments to/aware of who informed Castleside Echo. You should have made a note to clarify whether or not Heal was involved in the newspaper article. Asking this question would result in role actor response 8. I would urge caution as to how you frame questions of this nature. You do not want to give the impression that you are accusing Heal of any involvement.

1.3 ... why transferred to Castleside. You may want to build up a picture as to Heal's motivation for transferring to Castleside. Role actor response 7 would provide you with the information.

1.4 Suggests role actor contacts Castleside Echo to respond to article. Did you consider doing this when making your notes? After all, Heal is the team supervisor and has a better knowledge of the team. It would also show the team that Heal is supportive. Role actor response 10 would be delivered. There is a clear indication that the police view is not represented in the newspaper article. This shows the value of reading everything contained in a document. Had you failed to read the last paragraph you would not have had the opportunity to score this behavioural statement.

Area 2: Maximising Potential

This area contains four behavioural statements. Notice that 2.1 and 2.2 are prefixed by 'Acknowledges'. The scalar for this area is Thorough to Superficial.

2.1 ... role actor's past performance/experience. There are plenty of positives on which to focus as regards Heal's past performance and experience, as mentioned in Chief Inspector Venerdi's memorandum. In exercises of this nature, do not just focus on the negative aspects of a person's performance – identify the positive aspects and use them during your interaction.

2.2 ... role as supervisor/role model. Heal has a responsibility to the CSO team and this should be outlined. The team look to Heal for support and direction.

2.3 Asks role actor for views on role as CSO supervisor. Asking this question would result in role actor response 2. It would then be for you to further explore the content of that response. Doing that would result in you being awarded a higher scalar for this behavioural statement.

2.4 Encourages role actor to continue in role. Heal has a lot to offer the role. Their past experience suggests this is the case. You could suggest they continue as a response to you receiving role actor response 7. It is conceivable that this behavioural statement could be scored immediately after behavioural statement 1.3.

Area 3: Personal Responsibility

This area contains six behavioural statements, the maximum allowed for a competency area. Notice that 3.1 to 3.4 are prefixed by 'Informs role actor', and 3.5 and 3.6 prefixed by 'Outlines consequences'. The scalar for this area is Clear to Unclear.

3.1 ... that comments in canteen are unacceptable. Heal needs to be told that this is the case. The comments are unacceptable from any police officer, especially the person who is supervising the CSO team.

3.2 ... will speak to CSO Team. Did you make a note to do this? Heal's comment and the newspaper article have undermined the CSOs. You could do this to offer support or to address the comments in the newspaper article.

3.3 ... will monitor future conduct/comments. This is part of your role and you do not want a repeat of Heal's comment. Once again, be wary of how you frame your intention. You do not want to come across as being overbearing.

3.4 ... will investigate leaked report to press. Chief Inspector Venerdi's memorandum states that you should address the matters outlined. This includes the leaked information to the press. You could suggest that you are going to do this after confirming Heal was not involved.

3.5 ... of making comments in canteen. Outlining the perception members of staff now have of CSOs, the effect on CSO morale or personal consequences to Heal are examples of how this behavioural statement could be scored. I'm sure you identified other consequences to those I have mentioned.

3.6 ... of newspaper article. The newspaper article could affect CSO morale, give a poor impression of the police or affect the way CSOs are regarded by the community.

Area 4: Respect for Race and Diversity
This competency area does not contain behavioural statements. You are assessed across the five-minute interaction against two scalars, in this case Objective to Biased and Supportive to Unsupportive.

Merely focussing on the negative aspects of Heal's behaviour or supporting Heal's views of CSOs would lead you to be biased. In this exercise both Heal and the CSOs need your support. You are the divisional Inspector and have responsibility for both parties.

Candidate instructions

In this exercise you will receive four pages of preparatory information:

- a memorandum from Chief Inspector Venerdi
- a memorandum from Sergeant D Jeffries
- a report from P Khalid, HQ Corporate Development Department (two pages)

During the activity phase you will meet Sergeant D Jeffries.

CASTLESHIRE POLICE

Memorandum

From:	Chief Inspector Venerdi, Castleside
To:	Inspector 'Candidate', Castleside
Subject:	Attached memorandum from Sergeant D Jeffries
Date:	yesterday

Six months ago the force Motor Patrols Department was devolved to divisional responsibility. This was done after consultation with all key stakeholders including all ranks within the then Motor Patrols Department. Naturally some resistance was encounted, mostly, it has to be said, organised by Sergeant Jeffries. The Sergeant attended all of the discussion groups and was very vocal in their opinions.

Sergeant Jeffries stated that the safety of road users in the force area would be compromised once the department was devolved. This has not been the case with accident statistics remaining the same and in some areas slightly reduced. Sergeant Jeffries is a very well qualified and respected road traffic collision investigator and has been a key figure in successfully investigating a number of fatal road traffic collisions. The officer is qualified to the rank of Inspector.

The rationale behind devolving the department from central control was to deliver a better service to the division and provide each team within a division with specialist Fast Response Vehicles that would support divisional priorities. Consequently former members of the Motor Patrols Department now start at different police stations and operate on different radio channels.

Not only has this resulted in being more cost effective for the force, but it has also assisted in addressing divisional priorities. A small number of officers remain under central control to carry out duties with speed detection equipment to meet force priorities.

2

I am concerned with some of the issues Sergeant Jeffries has raised in his memorandum. I was not aware of these issues. I have emailed Sergeant Jeffries and arranged for the officer to meet you. The devolvement will not be reviewed.

I have attached some statistics which you may find useful.

L Venerdi

Chief Inspector

CASTLESHIRE

POLICE

CASTLESHIRE POLICE

Memorandum

From:	Sergeant D Jeffries, Castleside
To:	Chief Inspector Venerdi, Castleside
Subject:	Devolving of Motor Patrols
Date:	2 days ago

Sir,

It is now six months since the Motor Patrols Department was devolved, or should I say decimated, to divisions. I therefore thought it timely to give you an update as to how this has affected the former members of the department and how their skills are not being used to their best effect.

Communication between the now named 'Divisional Response Vehicles' is non-existent. On two occasions vehicles have refused to travel to Road Traffic Collisions as the collisions have not occurred in their division. This has left the control room confused as to who to send. It is obvious the control room is not fully clear as to the terms of reference for the vehicles. In fact, the cars and drivers are now viewed as glorified unit cars. Consequently, morale among the former members of the Motor Patrols Department is very low. I think it safe to say they no longer feel part of a team with specialist skills. As for myself, I have no supervisory responsibilities apart from overseeing investigations into fatal and serious road traffic collisions.

This leads me to my next point as to why I feel the devolvement process is not working. Such is the intransigence of divisions not allowing their cars to be used in other divisions that one officer at Castleside had to deal with and investigate three fatal Road Traffic Collisions in one week. How can that be deemed to be fair and the best use of resources? The sergeant with supervisory responsibility for that officer is not trained or qualified to offer any assistance to the officer. This could result in the loss of evidence.

Travelling time and costs going to and from their allocated police stations has increased for some officers as they were not allocated to the police station nearest to their home. This has also affected morale.

PASS FOR PROMOTION

2

It is therefore clear that this initiative cannot be allowed to continue and I respectfully request that the Castleside Divisional command team take up this situation with the force executive.

D Jeffries

Sergeant

CASTLESHIRE POLICE

Memorandum

From:	P Khalid, HQ Corporate Development Department
To:	Chief Inspector Venerdi, Castleside
Subject:	Latest Castleside Division Key Performance Statistics
Date:	2 days ago

I have attached the latest Castleside Division Key Performance Statistics.

Call handling management statistics (%)

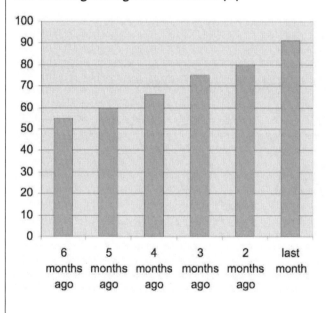

2

Take without owner's consent statistics

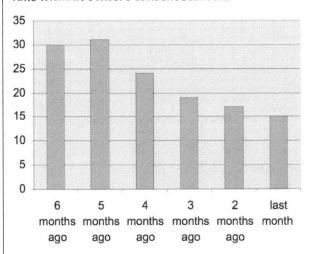

Theft from motor vehicle statistics

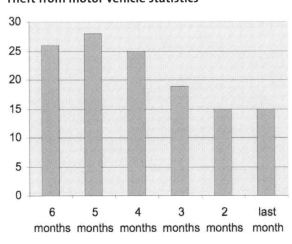

3

Fatal/serious Road Traffic Collision statistics

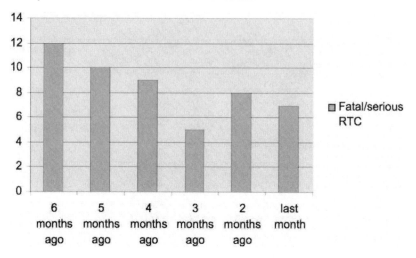

P Khalid

Force Statistics Officer

Candidate information debrief

What were your feelings when you read the exercise front cover and discovered that you had to read four pages of candidate information? There is a lot to read in this exercise, so you do not have time to waste.

I have tried to compile seven exercises that provide you with experience of using different document formats and examples of how the information can be delivered. For example, memorandums, emails and newspaper articles. This exercise contains performance information graphs.

This exercise is a good example of how you can address a person's beliefs or perceptions by using information contained within the documents contained in the exercise candidate information. It also contains examples of how information from one document can be linked to information contained in another.

Memorandum from Chief Inspector Venerdi

This memorandum does contain a lot of information for you.

The first paragraph informs you that six months ago the force Motor Patrols Department (MPD) was devolved to divisional responsibility. Did you consider at this point that the time scale might be relevant to the exercise? The opening paragraph then informs you that this was done in consultation with all key stakeholders, including members of the MPD. Sergeant Jeffries appears to have organised some resistance to the proposed changes. Did this information perhaps give you some insight into what your meeting with Jeffries may be about?

The second paragraph further outlines Jeffries' opposition to the changes. The paragraph also outlines that Jeffries is a well-respected, well-qualified Road Traffic Collision Investigator and is qualified to the rank of inspector.

The third and fourth paragraphs provide you with information as to the rationale for devolving the MPD and the consequences of such a change. You should have made notes in relation to these two paragraphs. I will address the information contained in them when we debrief the assessment checklist.

The memorandum then concludes with Chief Inspector Venerdi outlining their concerns about the content of Jeffries' memorandum. Significantly, the paragraph ends by pointing out that the devolvement will not be reviewed.

There is certainly a lot of information for you to contend with and digest in this memorandum, ranging from background about the devolvement to the actions of Sergeant Jeffries. However, as you will see in due course, it is valuable information you can use in your meeting with Jeffries.

Memorandum from Sergeant Jeffries

This is also a lengthy document for you to read and make your notes. However, as with Chief Inspector Venerdi's memorandum it contains important information for you. In fact you may agree that Jeffries does raise some valid points, points that you, as the divisional Inspector, will have to address.

The opening paragraph perhaps offers you a suggestion as to the content of the memorandum, particularly with the use of the word 'decimated' and a suggestion that officers' specific skills are being wasted.

Jeffries goes on to explain in the second paragraph that they believe there to be a serious problem with communications between the force control room and the Divisional Response Vehicles. How did you consider you could assist with this problem?

The paragraph then explains that morale among the former members of the MPD is now low. Jeffries morale is also low as they now have no supervisory responsibilities and their only focus appears to be overseeing fatal and serious Road Traffic Collisions. How did you consider you could assist with this problem?

In the next paragraph, Jeffries explains the problem encountered when divisions do not allow their Divisional Response Vehicle to assist in another division. Jeffries also highlights a problem one officer encountered when having to deal with three fatal Road Traffic Collisions in one week. Significantly perhaps, is the fact that the officer's sergeant was not trained or qualified to assist the officer. Did you consider how such a situation could be rectified? I will cover this point when we debrief the assessment checklist.

Jeffries then explains the problems some officers are facing since the changes were implemented. How did you consider you could assist with this problem?

Finally, Jeffries suggests that the devolvement should not be allowed to continue.

I appreciate that by now you must have identified a number of issues and lines of enquiry you feel you want to pursue during your meeting with Jeffries. And you only have five minutes.

Memorandum from P Khalid

The statistics relate to four everyday aspects of policing.

You will have no doubt noticed that all four graphs relate to performance over the last six months, since the MPD was devolved to division level. This is an example of linking information from the various sources in your candidate information. If you recall, the first paragraph of Chief Inspector Venerdi's memorandum informs you that the MPD was devolved to the divisions.

The graphs are fairly straightforward and I will focus more on their content when we debrief the assessment checklist. It will be of more benefit to you if we link the statistics to individual behavioural statements.

Role actor instructions

You are David/Dianne Jeffries, a sergeant with 12 years' service. You are qualified to the rank of inspector having passed the Part II assessment centre last year. You have spent the last seven years as a sergeant posted to the force Motor Patrols Department. You are very well qualified and respected as a Road Traffic Collision Investigator and have been a key figure in successfully investigating a number of fatal Road Traffic Collisions. You intend to apply to the next promotion boards scheduled in 10 months' time. You are married and live in Castleside.

Six months ago the Motor Patrols Department was taken out of central control and devolved to the divisions. You vigorously opposed this move and felt that the road users in the force area would suffer without a department dedicated to traffic matters and issues. You saw the move as little more than a cost cutting exercise. You were very happy with your role on the Motor Patrols Department.

Since the devolvement took place morale among the former Motor Patrols Officers has been low. They are no longer viewed as a specialist officer and consider themselves to be no more than a glorified fast response vehicle. They feel that their skills are no longer used to their best effect. You agree with this view. You no longer have any supervisory responsibility for the officers and are only called upon to supervise or assist at fatal or serious Road Traffic Collisions in a geographical area covering three divisions.

You feel that the devolving process has not worked. One reason being the intransigence of divisions in not allowing their cars to be used in other divisions. You are aware of one officer at Castleside who two months ago had to deal with and investigate three fatal Road Traffic Collisions that occurred in one week. You assisted this officer as best you could. The sergeant with supervisory responsibility for that officer was not trained or qualified to offer any assistance to the officer. You feel that this could result in the loss of evidence.

You are also aware that the time and costs of travelling to and from their allocated police stations has increased for some former Motor Patrols Officers as they were not allocated to the police station nearest to their homes. This has also affected morale.

You have not seen the latest statistics.

Demeanour: confident

When you enter the room, say:

1. **"Hello inspector I'm Sergeant David/Diane Jeffries. Chief Inspector Venerdi emailed me asking me to come and see you."**

   If the candidate asks what you want from the meeting, say:

2. **"I would like the command team at Castleside to take up the possibility of reviewing the situation regarding Motor Patrols with headquarters."**

   If the candidate asks why you opposed the devolving of the Motor Patrols Department, say:

3. **"I didn't think it was in the best interests of the road users or the officers."**

   If the candidate praises you for your skills/way you deal with fatal/serious Road Traffic Collisions, say:

4. **"Thanks for that inspector, but others have those skills too that I feel have been lost to the good of the force as a whole."**

   If the candidate outlines that the Motor Patrols Department was devolved so it would become more cost effective to the force, say:

5. **"At the end of the day it's not just about money. What about a quality of service to the road users and the officers involved?"**

   If the candidate outlines the statistics in relation to the call handling/take without owner's consent/theft from motor vehicle, say:

6. **"I appreciate that inspector, but that shows how the divisions are using the cars and drivers. They're just glorified response cars now."**

   If the candidate outlines the statistics in relation to the road traffic collision statistics, say:

7. **"That's only Castleside. I'd be interested to see what they're like across the force and in comparison to forces that haven't devolved their Motor Patrols."**

   If the candidate outlines that the decision to devolve Motor Patrols will not be reviewed, say:

8. **"I thought you might say that Inspector but I'm sure more long term they'll realise they made the wrong decision."**

   If the candidate suggests reviewing the allocation of officers' starting police stations, say:

9. "Well, it would be a step in the right direction."

    If the candidate suggests you use your skills/knowledge to assist divisional sergeants with Road Traffic Collisions, say:

10. "I could certainly do that, at least it would go some way to helping the investigation."

    If the candidate suggests meeting with former Motor Patrols Officers, say:

11. "If you think that will help."

    If the candidate suggests role actor could act as liaison with former Motor Patrols Officers, say:

12. "I could do that if you think it would help the situation."

    If the candidate asks you if you have any suggestions to improve morale of officers/address travelling issues/communication issues, say:

13. "Yes, by reinstating the Motor Patrols Department."

    If the candidate offers you assistance in preparing for promotion boards, say:

14. "I would appreciate that. I'm keen to get through first time."

Role actor instructions debrief

The exercise is not gender specific. Jeffries has 12 years' service and is qualified to the rank of inspector, having passed their Part II assessment centre last year and they intend to apply at the next promotion boards in 10 months' time.

The role actor instructions then outline details of Jeffries' background and their views on the devolvement of the Motor Patrols Department (MPD).

The remainder of the role actor instruction background is the same information as contained in Chief Inspector Venerdi's memorandum and Jeffries' memorandum. In the actual Part II assessment centre process, the role actors obtain the same information as that contained in the candidate information. This ensures that they all provide candidates with the same information. This ensures consistent delivery to all candidates and thereby ensuring fairness.

Jeffries has not seen the latest statistics. This is significant for you in the light of Jeffries' views on the devolvement and their opinion that it is unsuccessful.

The opening role actor response confirms Jeffries' identity to you and that Chief Inspector Venerdi has asked them to come and see you. It may be worth mentioning at this point that it can be confusing reading through an exercise containing three or four names. If you find yourself in the unfortunate position of having misread the candidate information and, for example, thought you were going to be meeting Chief Inspector Venerdi and in walks Jeffries, the only advice I can give is to not to panic, gather your thoughts and work your way through the candidate information.

Role actor response 2 outlines what Jeffries wants from your meeting with them. However, you are already aware from Chief Inspector Venerdi's memorandum that the devolvement will not be reviewed. So inform the role actor of this information.

Role actor response 3 would provide you with the opportunity to refer to the graph showing the road traffic collision statistics.

Role actor response 4 would provide you with the opportunity to point out that although MPD officers have been devolved to divisions, their skills have not been lost to the force.

Role actor response 5 is another opportunity for you to refer to the statistics to support the fact that devolvement has been successful.

Should you refer to the statistics relating to call handling, take without owners consent or theft from motor vehicle at any point during the interaction, role actor response 6 would be delivered. You may feel at this point that Jeffries is not going to move from their view of the devolvement. Do not be fazed by this but continue to respond to the role actor responses and refer to the candidate information. Remember, you do not have to resolve the issues in five minutes.

Role actor response 7 is specific to you having outlined the Road Traffic Collision statistics. The same advice applies as at role actor response 6.

Role actor response 8 again gives you the opportunity to outline the positive aspects of the devolvement.

Jeffries' memorandum clearly outlines that officer morale has been affected, not only by the devolvement, but by the allocation of police stations where officers start and finish their tour of duty. You are in a position, if not of altering their stations, then at least holding a review. Suggesting this would result in role actor response 9.

I will cover the points raised in the prompts for role actor response 10 when we debrief the assessment checklist. In this response Jeffries does strike a conciliatory tone.

Although you may feel that role actor responses 11 and 12 are quite bland and lacking in any enthusiasm from Jeffries, you should not be dismayed or feel that you are underachieving in the exercise.

Role actor response 13 is another opportunity to inform Jeffries that the MPD will not be restored to its previous format.

You may consider this final prompt in the script as a little out of keeping with the exercise. However, it clearly states in Chief Inspector Venerdi's memorandum that Jeffries is qualified for promotion. Jeffries does want to apply to the next promotion boards and, as one of your officers, should receive your support. Suggesting this would result in role actor response 14.

Assessment checklist

Competency Area	Scalar	Grade

Area 1: Planning and Organising
Outlines:

Scalar: **Purposeful – Vague** 1 2 3 4 5   Grade: A B C D

1.1 MPD devolved to provide better service
1.2 intention to meet with former MPD officers
1.3 intention to clarify use of vehicles with control room staff
1.4 intention to review officers' allocated stations

Area 2: Maximising Potential

Scalar: **Purposeful – Vague** 1 2 3 4 5   Grade: A B C D

2.1 Suggests role actor assists other sergeants
2.2 Outlines role actor is skilled/well respected Road Traffic Collision Investigator
2.3 Offers personal support re role actor's promotion

Area 3: Personal Responsibility
Outlines:

Scalar: **Thorough – Superficial** 1 2 3 4 5   Grade: A B C D

3.1 devolvement took place after consultation
3.2 devolvement will not be reviewed
3.3 call handling statistics have improved
3.4 TWOC statistics have improved
3.5 theft from motor vehicle statistics have improved
3.6 fatal/serious Road Traffic Collision statistics have improved

Area 4: Strategic Perspective
Outlines:

Scalar: **Thorough – Superficial** 1 2 3 4 5   Grade: A B C D

4.1 devolvement has been more cost effective
4.2 devolvement has assisted in addressing divisional priorities
4.3 officers still used to address force priority re speeding

Area 5: Respect for Race and Diversity

Scalar: **Sensitive – Insensitive** 1 2 3 4 5   Grade: A B C D

Supportive – Unsupportive 1 2 3 4 5

Assessment checklist debrief

The Jeffries exercise contains five competency areas; Planning and Organising, Maximising Potential, Personal Responsibility, Strategic Perspective and Respect for Race and Diversity.

The exercise contains 16 behavioural statements (statements a candidate should say). Remember there will be no more than six and no less than three behavioural statements in a competency area. Respect for Race and Diversity does not contain behavioural statements.

We will now take each competency area and behavioural statement in turn. Have your candidate information and role actor notes to hand to see which behavioural statements you would have scored.

Area 1: Planning and Organising
This area contains four behavioural statements. Notice all are prefixed by 'Outlines'. The scalar (how well a candidate scores the behavioural statements) for this area is Purposeful to Vague.

1.1 ... MPD devolved to provide better service. The candidate information contains information that you should use to address a person's beliefs or perceptions. This behavioural statement is an example. This information is contained in Chief Inspector Venerdi's memorandum.

1.2 ... intention to meet with former MPD officers. Jeffries outlines in their memorandum that morale amongst former MPD officers is low. This needs to be addressed. Meeting with the officers would go some way to addressing this.

1.3 ... intention to clarify use of vehicles with control room staff. Jeffries mentions in their memorandum that there are communication difficulties as control room staff are confused as to who to deploy to incidents. As the divisional Inspector, you are in a position to clarify this with control staff and their supervisors.

1.4 ... intention to review officers' allocated stations. Jeffries outlines in their memorandum the problem concerning officers' allocated police stations. Although you are not in a position to immediately change the situation as outlined, you could instigate a review process.

Area 2: Maximising Potential

This area contains three behavioural statements, the minimum number allowed in a competency area. The scalar for this area is Purposeful to Vague.

2.1 Suggests role actor assists other sergeants. This behavioural statement is an example of how linking information contained in the candidate information documents can be of benefit to you. The second paragraph of Chief Inspector Venerdi's memorandum outlines Jeffries' skills as a Road Traffic Collision Investigator. The third paragraph of Jeffries' memorandum points out that some sergeants do not possess these skills. Therefore, Jeffries could be used to assist. Did you identify both points in the memorandums and consider this as an option?

2.2 Outlines role actor is skilled/well respected Road Traffic Collision Investigator. This could be scored by focussing on the positive aspects of Jeffries' role, as outlined in the candidate information or even at the same time as scoring behavioural statement 2.1.

2.3 Offers personal support re role actor's promotion. Despite Jeffries' attitude towards the devolvement, Jeffries would still be appreciative of your support in preparing for the promotion boards.

Area 3: Personal Responsibility

This area contains four behavioural statements. Notice that all are prefixed by 'Outlines'. The scalar for this area is Thorough to Superficial.

3.1 ... devolvement took place after consultation. Jeffries believes that the devolvement should not have taken place. They also believe it has been to detriment of road users and officers. Role actor responses 2 and 3, as well as the contents of their memorandum, are a clear indication of this. To counter this belief you could use the information contained in Chief Inspector Venerdi's memorandum that the devolvement took place following consultation with key stakeholders, including all ranks in the MPD.

3.2 ... devolvement will not be reviewed. This is an example of why you should read all of the candidate information. This fact is located in the last sentence of the last paragraph of Chief Inspector Venerdi's memorandum and could easily be missed.

I want to look at behavioural statements **3.3 (... call handling statistics have improved), 3.4 (... TWOC statistics have improved), 3.5 (... theft from motor vehicle statistics have improved) and 3.6 (... fatal/serious Road Traffic Collision statistics have improved)** together as they are similar in nature. I mentioned earlier in the candidate information debrief that the graphs cover the period since the MPD was devolved. Jeffries believes that the initiative has been unsuccessful. Using the information contained in the graphs would address that perception. You could merely refer to the charts and say: 'Since the MPD was devolved the figures for call handling, TWOC, theft from motor vehicles and Road Traffic Collisions have all improved.' That one sentence would score all four behavioural statements. However, that would be a superficial way to score them and would probably warrant a scalar of 5 for each. If you consider the information each graph holds you could easily score all four on a much higher scalar by reading out the figures. Bear in mind that you are trying to convince Jeffries that the devolvement was successful, and quoting figures is a far more convincing argument than merely saying it has been successful. However, do not spend four minutes explaining graphs, there are other issues to address.

Area 4: Strategic Perspective

This area contains three behavioural statements: the minimum number allowed for a competency area. Notice that all are prefixed by 'Outlines'. The scalar for this area is Thorough to Superficial.

All three behavioural statements have their basis in addressing Jeffries' beliefs about the devolvement.

4.1 ... devolvement has been more cost effective. The fact outlined in this behavioural statement is contained in Chief Inspector Venerdi's memorandum. Role actor response 5 would be delivered once you had outlined this.

4.2 ... devolvement has assisted in addressing divisional priorities. The fact outlined in this behavioural statement is also contained in Chief Inspector Venerdi's memorandum.

4.3 ... officers still used to address force priority re speeding. The fact outlined in this behavioural statement is also contained in Chief Inspector Venerdi's memorandum.

Area 5: Respect for Race and Diversity

This competency area does not contain behavioural statements. You are assessed across the five-minute interaction against two scalars, in this case: Sensitive to Insensitive and Supportive to Unsupportive.

MCBURNIE

Candidate instructions

In this exercise you will receive two pages of preparatory information:

- a memorandum from Chief Inspector Venerdi
- a letter from Councillor McBurnie

During the activity phase you will meet Councillor B McBurnie.

CASTLESHIRE POLICE

Memorandum

From:	Chief Inspector Venerdi, Castleside
To:	Inspector 'Candidate', Castleside
Subject:	Attached letter from Councillor McBurnie
Date:	yesterday

I am sorry that I am not able to welcome you in person on your first day but I have to attend a Community Safety Strategy meeting at headquarters. I have just received a letter from Councillor McBurnie concerning under age drinking within Castleside.

Councillor McBurnie has worked closely with us and the community in establishing the designated 'alcohol free zone' within Castleside. The street drinking ban, which covers the Queens Road, Woodham Community School and Park area, gives powers to confiscate alcohol, bottles and glasses where it is believed a person poses a threat to public safety. Drinkers who refuse to co-operate can be arrested and face a fine up to £500.

I have checked with the communication centre for calls logged last Saturday. At 20.15 hours, an anonymous call was received from someone complaining about youths drinking in the Queens Road area. Anonymous calls of this nature are not categorised as high priority so no units attended.

Having been approved by the Castleside licensing committee, there is a lot of local interest to see if these schemes work. Councillor McBurnie's letter raises a number of issues, which causes me obvious concern and I would like to be kept updated. I have arranged for Councillor McBurnie to meet with you on your first day.

L Venerdi

Chief Inspector

Councillor B McBurnie
3 The Willows
Castleside
CS2 2TG

Date: Two days ago

Dear Chief Inspector Venerdi

As you aware, I am the parish councillor for the Woodham ward and a school governor at Woodham Community School. As such I take my responsibilities towards my community, the school and not least my family, very seriously.

Having worked closely with you to obtain the granting of the 'alcohol free zone', I am very disappointed that it appears that your officers are failing in their duties. Gangs of youths are blatantly ignoring the 'alcohol free zone' and getting away with it.

Last Saturday, youths aged between 13 and 15, built a den behind homes in the Queens Road area, near the school. After spending the evening drinking alcohol and causing misery to nearby residents, they left the area strewn with empty wine and spirit bottles and beer cans. I've received a complaint from a resident living in the Queens Road area who told me about a den. They had telephoned the police but no-one came out. Right outside this den is a sign warning that it is an alcohol-free area, but the youngsters just don't care.

I have become so incensed with this under-age drinking and that the police appear to be doing nothing to deal with these problems, I felt it necessary to do something about it myself. So last Wednesday, I arranged for my 13-year-old niece to see if she could buy alcohol from Cooper's Off-Licence in the High Street. Unsurprisingly, she was served without question.

I want to meet with you to discuss the lack of police action and so we can find a way to resolve these issues for the benefit of the whole community and deal once and for all with this loutish behaviour and lack of law enforcement.

B McBurnie
Councillor B McBurnie

Candidate information debrief

If you recall, when I described the exercise design process I mentioned that the exercises are based on actual policing incidents. The issues of youth disorder and anti-social behaviour are, as you are no doubt aware, everyday policing issues. They are issues that are dealt with regularly by inspectors performing uniform police duties.

The McBurnie exercise is the first non-police exercise in the series of seven. In this exercise you will meet a local councillor. Remember that no one exercise in the assessment process carries more weight than another, regardless of the role of the role actor.

On the surface this exercise appears to be quite straightforward: a local councillor who is unhappy with the lack of service provided by the police. However, there are other issues to address.

The candidate information is not as lengthy as the Jeffries exercise and consists of two documents; an internal memorandum and a letter.

Memorandum from Chief Inspector Venerdi

The opening paragraph explains why Chief Inspector Venerdi is unable to meet you on your first day and consequently with Councillor McBurnie. The paragraph provides you with an indication as to the possible content of McBurnie's letter.

The second paragraph of the memorandum provides you with background to the recently formed 'alcohol free zone' which covers the Queens Road, Woodham Community School and Park area of Castleside. The paragraph then outlines the powers relevant to the zone.

The memorandum then mentions an anonymous call received by the force communication centre last Saturday evening. No resources were dispatched as anonymous calls of this nature are not categorised as high priority. As a candidate I think that you would have correctly surmised that McBurnie's letter might refer to this incident.

The final paragraph outlines that there is a lot of local interest in the scheme. However, there are certain aspects of McBurnie's letter that cause the chief inspector some concern. As the divisional Inspector they should also cause you concern.

Letter from Councillor McBurnie

This is quite a lengthy letter but it does contain some useful information for you to use and issues that do need addressing.

The first paragraph informs you that McBurnie is the parish councillor for the Woodham ward and a school governor at the Woodham Community School. Did you consider that this information might be useful to you?

McBurnie then expresses dismay at the lack of police response to youths congregating in the 'alcohol free zone'. They are basing this assumption on the police response to one incident in particular.

The letter goes on to describe an incident involving youths aged between 13 and 15 years, who have constructed a 'den' beside a sign warning people that the area is an 'alcohol free zone'. The youths spent the evening drinking and left the area strewn with empty alcohol bottles and cans. A resident from Queens Road telephoned the police but no resources attended. This is obviously the same incident referred to in Chief Inspector Venerdi's memorandum.

The letter then describes action McBurnie has taken by using his 13-year-old niece to purchase alcohol at Cooper's Off-Licence. I am sure you made notes in relation to this and to how you would address this in your meeting with McBurnie.

The letter closes by outlining what McBurnie wants from the meeting.

As I stated at the beginning of the debrief, this is a straightforward everyday type of policing issue, revolving around youth disorder and anti-social behaviour.

Role actor instructions

You are Councillor Brendan/Beth McBurnie and you represent the Woodham ward on Castleside District Council. You are also a Governor at Woodham Community School. You have lived on the Woodham Estate for fourteen years and are married and have a daughter aged 14.

You have been a councillor for two years and have become extremely concerned about under age drinking and the anti-social behaviour associated with it. You worked closely with the police in obtaining the granting and powers for an 'alcohol free zone'. You have now written a letter outlining your concern that the police are failing in their duties in enforcing the 'alcohol free zone'.

Last Saturday, youths aged between 13 and 15, built a den behind homes in the Queens Road area, near the school. After spending the evening drinking and causing misery to nearby residents, they left the area strewn with bottles and cans. You received a complaint from a resident living in the Queens Road area who told you about the den. They had telephoned the police but no-one attended. Right outside this den is a sign warning that it is an alcohol-free area. There have been problems in the evenings and over weekends but you are not aware what calls have been made to the police. If asked, you will be willing to obtain details of witnesses.

You have become so incensed with this under-age drinking and that the police appear to be doing nothing to deal with these problems that you took it upon yourself to do something about it. Last Wednesday, you arranged for your 13-year-old niece to see if she could buy alcohol from Cooper's Off-Licence in the High Street. She purchased a bottle of cider and a pack of four alco-pops without being challenged.

Demeanour: confident

When you enter the room, say:

1. **"Hello inspector I'm Councillor Brendan/Beth McBurnie. You need to sort out this anti-social behaviour before it's too late."**

If the candidate asks what you want from the meeting, say:

2. **"It's as I've outlined in my letter: The 'alcohol free zone' has lost any credibility. If you don't sort this out soon, the community will do so."**

If the candidate asks you for details of the drinking den, say:

3. **"It's behind the houses in Queens Road near the Community School. The den is just an eyesore of empty bottles and cans."**

   If the candidate outlines the 'alcohol free zone' powers, say:

4. **"We have worked really hard to get these alcohol free zones. But these youths are still setting up dens and I dread to think what they are getting up to."**

   If the candidate asks if you have witnessed the drinking/seen the den/know the identity of the youths, say:

5. **"I don't know any of the youths but I'm sure they're local."**

   If the candidate asks about the off-licence test purchase, say:

6. **"They are obviously getting their alcohol locally and Cooper's Off-Licence clearly aren't helping matters."**

   If the candidate outlines risks with your test purchases/advises against taking matters into your own hands, say:

7. **"That may be so. But someone needs to take action and if this is what is required for you to take notice, then it has been worthwhile."**

   If the candidate asks if you are willing to work with the police, say:

8. **"I am more than happy to help in any way to make the streets safe again."**

   If the candidate states that they will make enquiries about the non-attendance following the call re the youths drinking in the den, say:

9. **"That's all well and good, but I'm more concerned about you dealing with the real issues."**

   If the candidate suggests arranging talking to the pupils/school/ parents, say:

10. **"That would be a start. I think your involvement could make a difference."**

    If the candidate suggests extra patrols to reassure the community/enforcing the 'alcohol free zone', say:

11. **"You have the powers and the resources. We just want the streets to be a safe place and not intimidating."**

    If the candidate suggests arranging a meeting with representatives from the council/school, say:

12. "If you think that will help. This needs sorting before someone gets hurt or suffers unnecessary harm."

Role actor instructions debrief

The exercise is not gender specific. McBurnie represents the Woodham ward on Castleside District Council. It could be useful to you that they are a governor at the local Woodham Community School.

McBurnie has been a councillor for the past two years and has worked closely with the police to set up the 'alcohol free zone'. You may feel that this fact is worth mentioning during your meeting with McBurnie.

The remainder of the role actor instructions background provides the role actor with the information contained in the candidate information.

The opening role actor response of the interaction confirms the role actor's identity. It also makes it clear to you how urgent McBurnie considers the situation to be.

Role actor response 2 confirms McBurnie's views as outlined in his letter but contains a comment that certainly requires a response from you, namely the intimation that the community intend to tackle the problem without the assistance of the police. How did you consider you would react to this information?

Role actor response 3 provides you with information of the drinking den. What options did you consider to address the problem outlined by McBurnie? You could consider short-term measures such as having the council remove the den as well as long-term measures such as addressing the problem via the local school.

Role actor response 4 would be delivered if you sought to reassure McBurnie that the police do have powers to address the youths.

I have mentioned previously about linking information from the candidate information and from the role actor. Role actor response 5 is an example of this. It contains information that you would find useful if used in conjunction with information from the candidate information. McBurnie mentions in their letter that the youths are aged between 13 and 15 years and the den has been constructed near the local Woodham Community School where the youths are likely to attend. McBurnie almost confirms this in role actor response 5, in which the belief is expressed that the youths are local. In the first paragraph of McBurnie's letter they inform you that they are a governor at this school. Linking this information from these different sources gives you the information to suggest an option of using the school to address the under age drinking problem.

At some point in the interaction you have to address the test purchase of alcohol McBurnie arranged at Cooper's Off-Licence. Role actor response 6 gives you some information.

Role actor response 7 follows on from you informing McBurnie of the risks involved in him making test purchases in the manner described.

Role actor response 8 outlines McBurnie's willingness to work with the police.

In order to reassure McBurnie you could offer to enquire into the result of the anonymous call regarding the youths. Role actor response 9 would follow.

Role actor response 10 would come as a result of you suggesting working with the school to address the under age drinking problem.

At some point you will make suggestions to address the problem, whether it be by initiatives such as Community Support Officers patrolling the area, police officers making arrests or sending letters to the youths' homes. Role actor response 11 would be your reply.

A more long-term strategy could be to arrange to meet with the council or school to discuss other measures to tackle the problem. Role actor response 12 would result.

Assessment checklist

Competency Area	Scalar	Grade
Area 1: Problem Solving **Asks role actor:** 1.1 for more details of drinking den 1.2 for details re identity of youths 1.3 for details re witnesses to under-age drinking **Suggest to role actor:** 1.4 meeting with the council/school/parents 1.5 intention to conduct test purchases	Thorough – Superficial 1 2 3 4 5	A B C D
Area 2: Community and Customer Focus **Explains:** 2.1 will arrange additional patrols in short term 2.2 intention to work with role actor/community re longer term issues/reassurance 2.3 the police will deal with all offenders appropriately 2.4 Acknowledges role actor's efforts in setting up 'alcohol free zone'	Clear – Unclear 1 2 3 4 5	A B C D
Area 3: Effective Communication **Informs role actor:** 3.1 will make enquiries re police non-attendance 3.2 that call to police was anonymous 3.3 to contact police re any further incidents/information 3.4 Outlines consequences of taking action without police support/knowledge	Purposeful – Vague 1 2 3 4 5	A B C D
Area 4: Respect for Race and Diversity	Objective – Biased 1 2 3 4 5 Supportive – Unsupportive 1 2 3 4 5	A B C D

Assessment checklist debrief

The McBurnie exercise contains four competency areas; Problem Solving, Community and Customer Focus, Effective Communication, and Respect for Race and Diversity.

The exercise contains 13 behavioural statements (statements a candidate should say). Remember that there will be no more than six and no less than three behavioural statements in a competency area. Respect for Race and Diversity does not contain behavioural statements.

We will now take each competency area and behavioural statement in turn. Have your candidate information and role actor notes to hand to see which behavioural statements you would have scored.

Area 1: Problem Solving
This area contains five behavioural statements. Notice that 1.1, 1.2 and 1.3 are prefixed by 'Asks role actor' and 1.4 and 1.5 are prefixed by 'Suggests to role actor'. The scalar (how well a candidate scores the behavioural statements) for this area is Thorough to Superficial.

1.1 ... for more details of drinking den. You should try to establish more details about the youths' drinking den. This will assist you to make an informed decision about your options to address the problem.

1.2 ... for details re identity of youths. McBurnie lives in the area. They are the local councillor and governor at the local school. Perhaps they have information that will assist you in identifying the youths.

1.3 ... for details re witnesses to under-age drinking. McBurnie mentions in their letter that a resident informed them about the drinking den. Do they have this person's details? Perhaps they could identify the youths.

1.4 ... meeting with the council/school/parents. I have already mentioned in the role actor instructions debrief in relation to role actor response 5 how you could use McBurnie's position as a governor to facilitate this suggestion.

1.5 ... intention to conduct test purchases. McBurnie has shown, albeit wrongly, that Cooper's Off-Licence is supplying alcohol to under age children. The police or local trading standards now need to conduct their own test purchases.

Area 2: Community and Customer Focus

This area contains four behavioural statements. Notice that 2.1, 2.2 and 2.3 are prefixed by 'Explains'. The scalar for this area is Clear to Unclear.

2.1 ... will arrange additional patrols in short term. The patrols could be by CSOs or high visibility police officers. Explaining why you intend doing this: to arrest/deter youths and to provide reassurance to community for example. This would achieve a higher scalar for this behavioural statement.

2.2 ... intention to work with role actor/community re longer term issues/reassurance. This is a longer-term strategy to address the problem and ensure compliance with the alcohol free zone regulations.

2.3 ... the police will deal with all offenders appropriately. Suggesting this would reassure McBurnie. The suggestion could be mentioned following role actor responses 1 or 2.

2.4 Acknowledges role actor's efforts in setting up 'alcohol free zone'. I mentioned in the role actor instructions debrief that this might be worth mentioning to McBurnie. Chief Inspector Venerdi mentions this in their memorandum. McBurnie's assistance should be recognised.

Area 3: Effective Communication

This area contains four behavioural statements. Notice that 1.1, 1.2 and 1.3 are prefixed by 'Informs role actor'. The scalar for this area is Purposeful to Vague.

3.1 ... will make enquiries re police non-attendance. This would reassure McBurnie that the police do take such calls seriously. Role actor response 9 would result.

3.2 ... that call to police was anonymous. It is conceivable that this behavioural statement could be scored immediately after behavioural statement 3.1. A higher scalar for this behavioural statement would be achieved if you went on to explain that in future any callers should provide their details.

3.3 ... to contact police re any further incidents/information. You need to work in partnership with McBurnie and the police need information from residents so they can react to any further problems.

3.4 Outlines consequences of taking action without police support/knowledge. This behavioural statement could refer to the information in role actor response 2 or to McBurnie conducting their own test purchase at Cooper's Off-Licence. The consequences could be residents putting themselves in danger or McBurnie or their niece being prosecuted for the test purchase.

Area 4: Respect for Race and Diversity

This competency area does not contain behavioural statements. You are assessed across the five-minute interaction against two scalars, in this case Objective to Biased and Supportive to Unsupportive.

Quite clearly McBurnie and the residents have a serious problem with youth disorder. A resident telephoned to report such an incident and the police did not attend. You would have to acknowledge this and apologise for police non-attendance. You do need to tackle the test purchase at Cooper's Off-Licence, but do not dwell on it too much and be sure to address it in a sensitive manner. You also need to be supportive to McBurnie and the residents.

Candidate Instructions

In this exercise you will receive three pages of preparatory information:

- a memorandum from Chief Inspector Venerdi
- a letter from S Stone
- a letter from S Perry

During the activity phase you will meet S Stone.

CASTLESHIRE POLICE

Memorandum

From: Chief Inspector Venerdi, Castleside
To: Inspector 'Candidate', Castleside
Subject: Cornforth Rehabilitation Centre
Date: yesterday

I have attached two letters regarding the proposed development of the Cornforth Rehabilitation Centre. The first is from a local resident S Stone, the second from the trust manager who will run the project, S Perry.

The Cornforth Rehabilitation Centre is the proposed site for a paedophile treatment centre. The centre will be run by a private trust funded by the Government. It has been set up after a pilot scheme elsewhere in the country showed a significant success rate in reducing re-offending. The offenders being treated at the centre are deemed to be low risk offenders. We have been involved in the initial meetings to set up the centre. We are satisfied that there is no significant risk to local residents and the trust have done all they can to eliminate any risk. The building is to be re-furbished and the centre will open in six months' time.

For your information the success rate to reduce re-offending on the pilot scheme was 80 per cent.

The attached letter from S Stone is self-explanatory. It is worth noting that a registered sex offender was forced to leave the area last month after attacks on his house. To date no-one has been arrested for this offence.

Unfortunately, I will be unable to meet with S Stone, as I will be out of the office for the next few days on a major incident exercise. I have arranged for them to meet with you.

L Venerdi

Chief Inspector

S Stone
21 Bethesda Street
The Meadows
Castleside
CS4 7TY

Date: Two days ago

Dear Chief Inspector Venerdi,

As a parent and resident of The Meadows area of Castleside I am writing to
you to express my disgust that the police are allowing the centre for sex
perverts to open on a housing estate. How can you let this happen? Is it
little wonder that residents on the estate now have little trust in the police?

The residents have formed an action committee and we are intent on
ensuring that this centre is not allowed to open. We have the support of our
local councillor who is going to put pressure on the council. The last thing
we want are these perverts preying on our children as they play or go to and
from school. It would be an understatement to say that feelings are running
high in the community. Some residents feel frustrated by the lack of action
and are considering taking matters into their own hands through various
methods. We are also planning a protest against the council's decision.

As you are aware, the building used to house these perverts was originally
earmarked by the council as a day nursery for local pre-school age children.
Little wonder then that this decision has caused even more resentment
amongst local residents. I appreciate that the area is classed as an area
identified for regeneration and that the majority of residents are low income
or unemployed but this decision just goes to show even more so that the
police and council do not care.

I want to meet you as soon as possible so we can try and sort out this
matter.

S Stone

The Bourn Trust

Mrs S Perry
The Bourn Trust
The Old Gatehouse
Windmill Lane
Linton
LN7 8JM

Re Cornforth Rehabilitation Centre

Dear Chief Inspector Venerdi, **Date:** three days ago

As you are aware the above centre has been approved by Castleside Council and is scheduled to open in six months. At our previous meetings we discussed the safety of people attending the centre for treatment and I expressed my concerns that you could not guarantee that they would not be harmed or the centre attacked.

It would now appear that those concerns were fully justified. Yesterday the project surveyor and her assistant attended the premises to carry out structural surveys to the property and inspect the rooms ahead of the commencement of the re-furbishment. When they arrived they saw that the sidewall had been daubed with obscene graffiti the content of which I have no desire to repeat. Basically it contained threats towards the building contractors and the future residents. To make matters worse, as she left the building she was subjected to a tirade of abuse from a man and a woman. These people threatened to damage her car and attack her should she return. Needless to say she is now frightened to carry out future work at the premises.

The reason for me writing to you is to alert you of the problems that lie ahead and for you to ensure that this project is allowed to go ahead as planned.

Yours sincerely,

S Perry

S Perry

Candidate information debrief

This is the second non-police exercise of three in the series of seven. It is another exercise that contains a lot of candidate information for you to read and make notes within the time constraints of the assessment centre.

How are you coping with managing the time constraints? If you feel you are still finding it difficult to read through the candidate information and make notes within the time constraints, do not be too concerned at this time. Continue to practice with the exercises. As in the actual assessment centre, put yourself under the 45 minute time constraints of the preparatory phase and work through all seven exercises consecutively. Don't forget to stop at 43 minutes and return to the first exercise to refresh your memory. Just as you would at the actual assessment centre. For extra practice use the seven exercises in the book that have been designed for candidates preparing for the constable to sergeant Part II assessment centre.

Memorandum from Chief Inspector Venerdi

The exercise concerns the proposed Cornforth Rehabilitation Centre that is being developed on the Meadows Estate in Castleside.

The memorandum provides you with background to the centre. The centre will be a rehabilitation centre for paedophiles and is to be managed by a private trust funded by the Government. A pilot scheme elsewhere in the country showed a significant success rate in reducing re-offending. The offenders attending the centre are deemed low risk. At this stage did you start to consider what the issues might be in the exercise? Perhaps you considered the issues would centre around a paedophile treatment centre opening on a local housing estate. But at this stage you have only read a small proportion of the candidate information. Do not form your opinion until you have read it all.

The memorandum then explains that Castleside Police have been involved in meetings to set up the centre and are satisfied that the public will not be at risk. The centre will open in six months.

The memorandum outlines that the pilot scheme reduced re-offending by 80 per cent. Did you identify this fact as being potentially useful to you?

The chief inspector then provides details of a registered sex offender whose home was attacked last month and who was forced to leave the area.

The memorandum concludes with a reason as to why the chief inspector will be unable to meet Stone. Always take note of information similar to this, as you may need to use it during your interaction with the role actor.

Letter from S Stone

The letter commences in quite a forceful tone with Stone outlining their disgust at the police for allowing, as they put it, a centre for 'sex perverts' to be opened on the estate. They also point out that the residents now have little trust in the police. The two comments that should cause you concern and for you to address in this paragraph are as follows; the 'sex perverts' comment, which I will cover when we debrief the role actor instructions, and the lack of trust the residents now have in the police.

The letter continues in the same vein outlining that an action committee has been formed and the local councillor has backed the campaign. Did you consider how this information might be useful to you?

Stone then points out that residents are fearful of attacks on children. Alarmingly, feelings are running high in the community with some residents considering taking matters into their own hands. A protest is also planned. As you no doubt appreciate, and probably made notes to that effect, you need to act on this information at the earliest opportunity.

Finally, the letter gives you information that the building was originally earmarked for a day nursery for local children of pre-school age. The change of plan has only fuelled resentment on the estate. The letter ends by pointing out that there is a belief on the estate that the police and council do not care about the estate.

The letter provides you with a clear indication as to the issues Stone wishes to discuss with you. It contains a number of beliefs and perceptions that you will need to address in your meeting. However, as you will see when we debrief the role actor instructions and assessment checklist you have the information to address those beliefs and perceptions.

Letter from S Perry

Perry is the representative of The Bourn Trust, the organisation which will have responsibility for managing the centre when it opens.

The letter explains that contractors recently attended the site and were subject to verbal abuse and threats to damage their vehicle from a man and a woman at the scene. The result is that the female project surveyor is now frightened to return to the site. The letter also points out that the side wall of the building had been daubed with obscene graffiti. What did you consider in relation to this information?

The letter concludes with Perry more or less suggesting that the police should be prepared for future problems of this nature and that the support of the police will be required if the project is to go ahead.

So there you have it, a local resident with the support of the community who wants the centre development stopped, the other requesting police support to ensure it goes ahead as approved and planned.

Role actor instructions

You are Sam/Sarah Stone, a resident of The Meadows housing estate. You live there with your partner and two year old son. You work as a cleaner at the local primary school. You have lived on the estate for the past five years. The area is classed as an area identified for regeneration and the majority of the residents are on low incomes or unemployed.

Until two months ago, the council had identified a disused building as a suitable site for a day nursery for pre-school children. You intended to send your own son to the nursery. You were delighted by this decision as it would help you and your partner with childcare arrangements. Many other parents on the estate also welcomed the decision. However, a month ago the council announced it had reversed its decision and had sold the property to The Bourn Trust to use as a paedophile rehabilitation centre. This decision has caused outrage on the estate as residents already believe that the council sees them as second-class citizens. The residents are also shocked that the police would allow the opening of this type of premises. Feelings on the estate are running high. You have formed an action committee in a bid to put pressure, through your local councillor and the police, on the council to reverse its decision and open the day nursery instead. Some residents are feeling frustrated that this course of action is not bringing results, so they are threatening to take matters in their own hands.

Trust in the police and council has been eroded by the decision to open the centre. The residents see this as another example of lack of care about the estate.

A protest is in the process of being planned but the final details are yet to be finalised.

A month ago a registered sex offender was forced to leave the estate after his house was attacked. You do not know who is responsible for this attack.

You do not know who is responsible for causing damage to the building or threatening the staff from The Bourn Trust.

Demeanour: annoyed

When you enter the room, say:

1.   **"Hello inspector I'm Sam/Sarah Stone. I was hoping to see the chief inspector about this problem."**

If the candidate explains why Chief Inspector Venerdi cannot see you, say:

2. **"Well there's another example of how much you care about our estate."**

    If the candidate reassures you that the police are concerned about the estate, say:

3. **"Well you wouldn't think it. Allowing this home for perverts to go ahead."**

    If the candidate outlines it was a council decision to allow the home to be built, say:

4. **"Yes but the police could have put a stop to it by objecting."**

    If the candidate outlines that only offenders deemed as low risk will attend the centre, say:

5. **"But what guarantees can you give us that these people won't prey on our children?"**

    If the candidate outlines the 80 per cent success rate in preventing re-offending for the scheme, say:

6. **"Figures mean nothing. That's still 20 per cent who attack children."**

    If the candidate outlines that the police are satisfied there is no significant risk to local residents, say:

7. **"You are bound to say that. But if any children are attacked, try and justify that opinion then."**

    If the candidate asks if you know the identity of the people who attacked the sex offender's house/threatened the staff from The Bourn Trust/damaged the building, say:

8. **"No I don't and I doubt anyone will tell you since no-one trusts you on the estate."**

    If the candidate outlines that people should not take matters into their own hands, say:

9. **"It's fine for you to say that. How would you feel if a centre like this was opening in your street? "**

    If the candidate points out the consequences of people taking matters into their own hands, say:

10.   "I really think they don't care. Feelings are running so high at the moment."

If the candidate suggests a meeting with police/residents/The Bourn Trust/council, say:

11.   "If you think that will help then you can give it a go."

If the candidate suggests having a Community Beat Manager/Community Support Officers for reassurance/build up trust on estate, say:

12.   "That may go someway towards helping us."

If the candidate asks for details of the planned protest, say:

13.   "We haven't decided on all the details but I expect a lot of people, particularly women and children, will turn up."

Role actor instructions debrief

The exercise is not gender specific. The opening paragraph outlines details of Stone's background and the nature of The Meadows estate.

As with all role actor instructions, the remainder of the background provides the role actor with the information contained in the candidate information. As I have mentioned previously this ensures consistency in the role actor's delivery to all candidates.

The opening role actor response confirms the role actor's identity and suggests that Stone was hoping to meet with Chief Inspector Venerdi.

You have the information in the Chief Inspector's memorandum as to why they cannot be present.

Having informed Stone of this, you would receive role actor response 2. How would you react to this? Hopefully by reassuring Stone that the police do care about the estate. This would then be met with role actor response 3.

Stone refers to the people attending the centre as 'sex perverts'; you should challenge Stone about the use of inappropriate language but do so within the bounds of Respect for Race and Diversity.

Role actor response 3 also suggests that the police are allowing the home to go ahead. You could use the information in Chief Inspector Venerdi's memorandum that the police were involved in the initial meetings but are not wholly responsible for the centre going ahead. This would result in role actor response 4.

To address Stone's perceptions you should use the information relating to the fact the offenders are deemed low risk, this would result in role actor response 5 and that re-offending on the pilot scheme was reduced by 80 per cent, as mentioned in Chief Inspector Venerdi's memorandum, role actor response 6 would then be delivered. I'm sure you will agree that both role actor responses are confrontational but the important thing is to use the candidate information to address Stone's perceptions. You may feel with this exercise that you are in a no win situation, but as I have mentioned previously, you do not have to resolve these exercises in five minutes.

Role actor response 7 is similar. You have again used the candidate information to address Stone's perceptions.

The exercise does contain information relating to offences that have taken place. Stone lives on the estate, do they know who is responsible? Role actor response 8 clearly informs you they do not but it also informs you that trust in the police has been eroded. This confirms the comment in Stone's letter. You need to consider how you can address this.

There is clear indication in Stone's letter that residents plan on taking matters into their own hands. The residents need to be persuaded that they should not follow this route. Role actor response 9 would result. How would you react to this comment? Remember you must remain impartial throughout the five-minute interaction.

Role actor response 10 would be delivered after you point out the consequences of residents taking matters into their own hands. Again you may feel as though you have wasted your time as the response is quite dismissive. Do not be dismayed; the key factor is you have mentioned the consequences.

Role actor response 11 follows your suggestion of meeting with one or all of the parties involved.

As we have already highlighted, you need to build up trust on the estate. The suggestions in the prompt for role actor response 12 are examples of how this can be done.

You need details of the planned project as mentioned in Stone's letter as you may need to provide resources to police it. Role actor response 13 provides you with the details.

As you will have gathered, the Stone exercise has a confrontational role actor. This should not faze you. Listen to what they have to say and continue to use your candidate information and you will address their concerns.

Assessment checklist

Competency Area	Scalar	Grade

Area 1: Problem Solving
Asks role actor:
Thorough – Superficial
1 2 3 4 5
A B C D

1.1 for details of planned protest
1.2 know who attacked sex offender's house
1.3 know who damaged centre building
1.4 know who threatened The Bourn Trust staff
1.5 if aware of results of pilot scheme

Area 2: Community and Customer Focus
Explains:
Thorough – Superficial
1 2 3 4 5
A B C D

2.1 pilot scheme was a success
2.2 pilot scheme reduced re-offending by 80 per cent
2.3 only low risk offenders attend centre
2.4 concerned at lack of trust in police

Area 3: Effective Communication
Outlines:
Purposeful – Vague
1 2 3 4 5
A B C D

3.1 attacks/threats to any person unacceptable
3.2 residents must not take matters into own hands
3.4 consequences of residents taking matters into own hands (arrest/prosecution)
3.4 residents have right to peaceful protest

Area 4: Personal Responsibility
Outlines intention:
Purposeful – Vague
1 2 3 4 5
A B C D

4.1 to attend meeting with residents
4.2 to work together with residents
4.3 to investigate damage/threats
4.4 to investigate alternative premises for day nursery

Area 5: Respect for Race and Diversity
Objective – Biased
1 2 3 4 5
Sensitive – Insensitive
1 2 3 4 5
A B C D

Assessment checklist debrief

The Stone exercise contains five competency areas; Problem Solving, Community and Customer Focus, Effective Communication, Personal Responsibility and Respect for Race and Diversity.

The exercise contains 17 behavioural statements (statements a candidate should say), only one short of the maximum allowed for an exercise. Remember there will be no more than six and no less than three behavioural statements in a competency area. Respect for Race and Diversity does not contain behavioural statements.

We will now take each competency area and behavioural statement in turn. Have your candidate information and role actor notes to hand to see which behavioural statements you would have scored.

Area 1: Problem Solving

This area contains five behavioural statements. Notice that all are prefixed by 'Asks role actor'. The scalar (how well a candidate scores the behavioural statements) for this area is Thorough to Superficial.

1.1 ... for details of planned protest. As I mentioned in the role actor instructions debrief, you need to be aware of this information to plan any police response that may be required.

1.2 ... know who attacked sex offender's house. Did you identify this information in Chief Inspector Venerdi's memorandum? Stone may have information regarding this offence. Asking this question would result in role actor response 8.

1.3 ... know who damaged centre building. This is similar to behavioural statement 1.2. The information regarding the damage is contained in Perry's letter. Asking this question would also result in role actor response 8.

1.4 ... know who threatened The Bourne Trust staff. This is similar to behavioural statements 1.2 and 1.3. The information regarding the threats is contained in Perry's letter. Asking this question would also result in role actor response 8.

1.5 ... if aware of results of pilot scheme. Stone may already be aware of the results, however, you could clarify this before referring to the information.

Area 2: Community and Customer Focus

This area contains four behavioural statements. Notice that all are prefixed by 'Explains'. The scalar for this area is Thorough to Superficial.

2.1 ... pilot scheme was a success. You need to address Stone's concerns regarding the people attending the centre. You would do this by referring to the contents of the candidate information. The success of the pilot scheme is contained in Chief Inspector Venerdi's memorandum.

2.2 ... pilot scheme reduced re-offending by 80 per cent. This figure would also assist in addressing Stone's concerns. You would have to actually quote the figure to score the behavioural statement. The figure is contained in Chief Inspector Venerdi's memorandum. Role actor response 6 would follow.

2.3 ... only low risk offenders attend centre. This information would also assist in addressing Stone's concerns. This information is also contained in Chief Inspector Venerdi's memorandum. Role actor response 5 would follow.

2.4 ... concerned at lack of trust in police. You could express your concern by referring to the information regarding the lack of trust mentioned in Stone's letter or by responding to role actor response 8.

Area 3: Effective Communication

This area contains four behavioural statements. Notice that all are prefixed by 'Outlines'. The scalar for this area is Purposeful to Vague.

3.1 ... attacks/threats to any person unacceptable. This would refer to attacks or threats to The Bourn Trust staff and/or sex offenders.

3.2 ... residents must not take matters into own hands. Stone should be informed that this should not take place.

3.3 ... consequences of residents taking matters into own hands (arrest/prosecution). This behavioural statement should follow on from behavioural statement 3.2. Examples of consequences could be arrest or loss of public sympathy.

3.4 ... residents have right to peaceful protest. You are aware that a protest is planned. Stone should be informed that this is their right. However, the protest must be peaceful.

Area 4: Personal Responsibility

This area contains four behavioural statements. Notice that all are prefixed by 'Outlines intention'. The scalar for this area is Thorough to Superficial.

4.1 ... to attend meeting with residents. You need to do this for two reasons; address the residents' perceptions of the centre and pass on the information outlined in Chief Inspector Venerdi's memorandum and to address the lack of trust in the police. Mentioning both would achieve a high scalar for this behavioural statement.

4.2 ... to work together with residents. You could become the police contact for the residents and assist them with any queries they have concerning the centre. This would also help to restore some of the trust in the police. Remember you are the inspector responsible for the area.

4.3 ... to investigate damage/threats. Offences have been committed and need to be investigated. You are in a postion to ensure this is carried out. This behavioural statement would cover offences committed against the sex offender who was forced to leave the area and offences at the site of the development.

4.4 ... to investigate alternative premises for day nursery. It states in Stone's letter that the building was earmarked for use as a day nursery. Offering your assistance to liaise with the council would address Stone's belief that the police do not care about the estate and assist in addressing the lack of trust in the police. I have included this behavioural statement to emphasise to you the importance of reading all of the candidate information. The information about the day nursery could easily be dismissed as irrelevant.

Area 5: Respect for Race and Diversity

This competency area does not contain behavioural statements. You are assessed across the five-minute interaction against two scalars, in this case Objective to Biased and Sensitive to Insensitive.

You need to remain impartial throughout the five-minute interaction and sensitive to the needs of all parties.

Candidate instructions

In this exercise you will receive three pages of preparatory information:

- A memorandum from Chief Inspector Venerdi
- A letter from A Tijani
- Copy of a leaflet

During the activity phase you will meet A Tijani.

CASTLESHIRE POLICE

Memorandum

From: Chief Inspector Venerdi, Castleside
To: Inspector 'Candidate', Castleside
Subject: Attached letter from A Tijani
Date: yesterday

I have attached a letter from A Tijani, one of the key members of the Castleside multi-racial community forum. A Tijani represents the interests of the asylum seeker community on the forum and is well respected in the community. The forum has representatives from the council, housing trusts, local charities and social services. The forum has been in operation for the past 12 months.

We have worked very hard to build up ties within the asylum seeker community and I do not wish to see them undermined. As you are the police representative at the forum, I thought it important that you meet with them as soon as possible, so I have arranged for A Tijani to meet you.

Personally, I have no knowledge of the organisation 'Britain for Britons' mentioned in the letter nor any knowledge of the incident involving the two officers.

L Venerdi

Chief Inspector

A Tijani
7 Holly Road
Castleside
CS2 5FH

Date: two days ago

Dear Chief Inspector Venerdi,

I hope that by writing this letter you do not feel that I am circumventing the usual procedures that we follow via our forum. I feel it necessary to take this course of action as I do not wish to cause your police representative any embarrassment at the next meeting.

As you are only too aware, the asylum seeker hostel is now well established. However, it would appear that still some members of the community have not accepted this and neither would it appear have some of your officers. I thought we had improved the knowledge of and attitudes towards asylum seekers by your officers through our earlier initiatives. This does not seem to be the case.

I have only just been informed by our support worker at the hostel of an incident that occurred two days ago when two of your officers attended the hostel to take a report of theft from a male resident. The man is an Iraqi who left the country to avoid political persecution. He has a job at a local warehouse and pays for his accommodation at the hostel. However, his English is somewhat limited and he had difficulty explaining to the officers what had happened. Basically he had been robbed and his wages stolen. Quite naturally he was distressed and unable to communicate properly. Unfortunately, the support worker was not present in the hostel to assist. As the officers were leaving the hostel, one of the residents overheard one of them say to the other officer, 'He's only upset because he's lost his state handout that you and I pay for'.

Nothing could be further from the truth, which brings me to my next concern: the misinformation being circulated by a group calling itself 'Britain for Britons'. The view voiced by your officer is just the kind of myth been circulated by this group in the Castleside area. If this attitude is allowed to take root, and I believe it already has, I can only imagine what may follow. I have attached a copy of their leaflet for your information.

A Tijani

A Tijani

The truth about what's really happening in YOUR community

FACT! Refugees sponge off the state:

Your taxes are being diverted to pay for the scroungers. Council taxes are increased to keep them in their warm hostel.

FACT! Refugees see us as the land of milk and honey:

All asylum seekers come here because they know we are a soft touch and they can live off the state. They are not interested in working.

FACT! Refugees prey on residents:

Asylum seekers commit more crime than the people who already live in an area. The old and young are easy targets for them.

FACT! Refugees get priority treatment and housing:

Did you know they have their own forum supported by YOUR police and council? What do you think gets discussed behind those closed doors?

If you've had enough of being a second-class citizen join us now and fight for equality.

BRITAIN FOR BRITONS

Candidate information debrief

This is the third and final non-police exercise in the series. As you are now aware it relates to the topical issue of asylum seekers.

Although the candidate information comprises of three pages, the page containing the leaflet is not only included for your information; as you will see in due course, there are behavioural statements that refer to it.

Memorandum from Chief Inspector Venerdi

Although quite short in content, the memorandum provides you with useful background information to prepare you for your meeting with Tijani.

The first paragraph informs you that Tijani is one of the key members on the Castleside multi-racial community forum. They represent the interests of the local asylum seeker community. The forum is a multi-agency forum and has operated for the past 12 months. This paragraph is useful in that it sets the scene and, crucially perhaps, informs you that Tijani represents the local asylum seeker community.

The memorandum continues with the chief inspector expressing concern that they do not want to see ties within this community undermined. Clearly an incident has occurred that has caused them to mention this.

The memorandum ends with mention of an organisation called 'Britain for Britons' and an incident involving two police officers.

Letter from A Tijani

The letter commences by intimating that an incident has occurred which Tijani feels may cause the police embarrassment if mentioned in a public forum. This should immediately cause you concern.

The letter then explains that Tijani feels that the community in general is prejudiced towards the asylum seekers. Alarmingly, it appears so are some police officers, despite an earlier initiative to improve officers' knowledge and attitudes towards the asylum seekers. Did you make a note to enquire with Tijani what those initiatives were made up of?

The letter then describes an incident involving two police officers and an asylum seeker who was the victim of a robbery. One of the officers was heard to make an inappropriate comment about the asylum seeker. I am certain you made comprehensive notes regarding this incident, particularly in relation to the officer's attitude and the investigation of the offence itself. I will refer to the contents of this paragraph in more depth when we debrief the assessment checklist.

Tijani then outlines their concern regarding a leaflet that is circulating around the Castleside area. Tijani is concerned about the impact this leaflet could have on not only the asylum seeker community but also the local community in general. You should share those concerns when you consider the potential result of allowing the leaflet to circulate.

Leaflet from 'Britain for Britons'

This document has provided you with experience of using a document of this nature and is another example of how information could be presented to you.

No doubt you will have gathered that it is extremely racially inflammatory and will have consequently made a note of the potential implications this document could have on the asylum seekers and the local community. You should also have made notes outlining how you intend to address the leaflet and its contents. I will cover this in more depth when we debrief the assessment checklist.

Role actor instructions

You are Alex/Alexis Tijani. You are of Yugoslavian origin and came to Britain during the Balkan conflict in the 1980s. You are not married and live in Castleside. You have lived here since you came to Britain. You are the Castleside council representative for asylum seekers. You are well respected in the community.

There are currently 200 asylum seekers residing in Castleside. There is no tension between residents and asylum seekers. In fact relations are good. The Castleside multi-racial community forum has helped this. The forum was established 12 months ago and includes representatives from the council, police, housing trusts, local charities and social services. You represent the asylum seeker community. The Castleside Inspector represents the police. The forum meets every four weeks. The next meeting is in two weeks.

Some of the asylum seekers, 50 in total, reside in a hostel. When the hostel was proposed, it was met with some resistance by the local community but holding forums and meetings within the community and reaching out to community groups overcame this. Lately, however, you have noticed a shift in attitude by some local residents towards the hostel and the asylum seekers in general. You believe a group calling itself 'Britain for Britons' distributing racially inflammatory leaflets in the area may have caused this. The group seems to target the poorer areas in the community. You do not have any information about the members of the group or where they meet. You have overheard comments in the community echoing those on the leaflet.

Two days ago, a support worker at the asylum seeker hostel told you of an incident involving an Iraqi man and two police officers. The man had been robbed on his way home from work and his wages stolen. He was very distressed and consequently was unable to communicate very well with the police officers. However as the officers were leaving, another resident overheard them say, 'He's only upset because he's lost his state handout that you and I pay for'. You do not have any further details of the robbery.

You thought this comment unacceptable and that officers' perceptions of asylum seekers had been addressed by a series of presentations you gave to officers 10 months ago.

Demeanour: confident

When you enter the room, say:

1.   **"Hello inspector I'm Alex/Alexis Tijani. Thank you for seeing me."**

If the candidate asks what you want from the meeting, say:

2.   **"It is as outlined in my letter."**

If the candidate asks you for details of the two officers at the hostel, say:

3.   **"I don't know who they are but I was very surprised by one of them and his comment."**

If the candidate asks if you want to make a formal complaint about the officer, say:

4.   **"No I don't inspector. I just want you to do something about it."**

If the candidate asks if the Iraqi man wants to make a formal complaint, say:

5.   **"No he doesn't. He just wants the police to do something about it."**

If the candidate asks what you did in earlier initiatives with officers, say:

6.   **"I delivered some presentations to help the officers and addressed some of the myths surrounding asylum seekers."**

If the candidate apologises for the comment/states comment unacceptable, say:

7.   **"I hope this view is not one held widely by your officers and that you don't just attend the forums to pay lip service."**

If the candidate outlines they will find out which officer made comments/investigate comments, say:

8.   **"That's a matter for you but they should not be making these unfounded comments."**

If the candidate asks if you have any details of the group 'Britain for Britons', say:

9.   **"I don't, but they appeared on the scene about two months ago apparently."**

If the candidate outlines intention to investigate/make further enquiries about 'Britain for Britons' group, say:

10. **"That's good, before they cause real harm in the community."**

If the candidate asks you where you got the leaflet, say:

11. **"It was handed to me by a resident at the hostel who found it in the street. They were very concerned about the lies in it."**

If the candidate outlines an intention to meet with residents of the hostel, say:

12. **"That would go some way to addressing their concerns."**

If the candidate outlines an intention to have the robbery of Iraqi man investigated/other officers attend, say:

13. **"I appreciate that, but it could have been handled better in the first instance."**

Role actor instructions debrief

The exercise is not gender specific. Tijani is of Yugoslavian origin and has resided in Britain since the 1980s having lived in Castleside since their arrival.

The role actor instructions background then outlines details of the asylum seeker community in Castleside and the multi-racial forum, which meets every four weeks.

Tijani has recently noticed a shift in attitude by some local residents towards the asylum seekers. They believe this has been caused by the distribution of the leaflet contained in the exercise candidate information.

The background then provides the role actor with details of the incident involving the two officers. Tijani held a series of presentations 10 months ago to address officers' perceptions.

Role actor response 1 confirms the role actor's identity. It also strikes a conciliatory note.

Role actor response 2 merely confirms that they have requested the meeting to address the issues outlined in their letter. Therefore, you can surmise that no other issues will arise during the meeting. However, still be prepared to react to the role actor responses.

No doubt you intend to investigate the incident involving the officers. Perhaps Tijani is aware of their identity. Chief Inspector Venerdi's memorandum does not identify the officers. Role actor response 3 provides you with the information Tijani possess.

Role actor responses 4 and 5 inform you that neither Tijani, nor the robbery victim, wishes to make a complaint relating to the officer's actions. However, both responses clearly indicate that they want you to address the matter.

The fact that Tijani has made the presentations mentioned is contained in their letter. You need details of these presentations as you may consider that another initiative is required to address officers' attitudes. Role actor response 6 provides you with the information.

Role actor response 7 provides you with the opportunity to reassure Tijani that you believe the view they have expressed is not the case. To provide further reassurance, you could inform Tijani that you intend to conduct an investigation into the incident. That suggestion would provide role actor response 8.

At some point during the interaction you need to turn your attention to the group calling itself 'Britain for Britons'. You are new to the area whereas Tijani works within the community. Asking if they have any information regarding the group would result in the delivery of role actor response 9.

You should have made a note to investigate the leaflet and/or the 'Britain for Britons' group. Outlining your intention to do this to Tijani would result in role actor response 10.

You may consider that Tijani can also provide some information regarding the leaflet that is circulating in the community. Role actor response 11 would provide you with some information.

Clearly the attitude of the two officers has had an affect on the hostel residents. As the person responsible for the division, one of your responsibilities should be to ensure that the hostel residents are reassured. Suggesting such a meeting would result in role actor response 12.

There is no indication that the robbery of the Iraqi man has been fully and correctly investigated. You need to ensure that officers carry this out to the standard that is expected. Outlining your intention to ensure this takes place would result in role actor response 13. This response could lead to you outlining your intention to speak to the two officers who attended the report of the robbery.

Assessment checklist

Competency Area	Scalar	Grade
Area 1: Problem Solving **Asks role actor:** 1.1 if know identity of officers 1.2 what were initiatives with officers 1.3 if want to make complaint/robbery victim wants to make complaint 1.4 what were comments heard in community	Thorough – Superficial 1 2 3 4 5	A B C D
Area 2: Community and Customer Focus **Outlines:** 2.1 will update role actor regarding officers 2.2 will update role actor regarding leaflets/ group 2.3 intention to meet with hostel residents	Thorough – Superficial 1 2 3 4 5	A B C D
Area 3: Personal Responsibility **Outlines:** 3.1 officer's comments unacceptable 3.2 will find out identity of officer 3.3 will speak to/deal with officer 3.4 intention to speak to other teams 3.5 intention to investigate leaflet/group 3.6 intention to investigate robbery of asylum seeker	Purposeful – Vague 1 2 3 4 5	A B C D
Area 4: Strategic Perspective **Outlines:** 4.1 personal commitment to forum 4.2 organisational commitment to forum 4.3 leaflet is racially motivated/racial incident 4.4 potential implications of leaflet	Purposeful – Vague 1 2 3 4 5	A B C D
Area 5: Respect for Race and Diversity	Objective – Biased 1 2 3 4 5 Sensitive – Insensitive 1 2 3 4 5	A B C D

Assessment checklist debrief

The Tijani exercise contains five competency areas; Problem Solving, Community and Customer Focus, Personal Responsibility, Strategic Perspective and Respect for Race and Diversity.

The exercise contains 17 behavioural statements (statements a candidate should say), only one short of the maximum allowed for an exercise. Remember there will be no more than six and no fewer than three behavioural statements in a competency area. Respect for Race and Diversity does not contain behavioural statements.

We will now take each competency area and behavioural statement in turn. Have your candidate information and role actor notes to hand to see which behavioural statements you would have scored.

Area 1: Problem Solving
This area contains four behavioural statements. Notice that all are prefixed by 'Asks role actor'. The scalar (how well a candidate scores the behavioural statements) for this area is Thorough to Superficial.

1.1 ... if know identity of officers. As I mentioned in the role actor instructions debrief, you need to establish the identity of the officers concerned in order to take whatever action you consider necessary.

1.2 ... what were initiatives with officers. Asking this would help establish what has been done to address all officers' knowledge and attitudes. This information would assist you in making an informed decision as to how you feel this could be further progressed.

1.3 ... if want to make complaint/robbery victim wants to make complaint. Tijani and/or the robbery victim may feel that the officer's attitude was such that it warrants a complaint. Role actor responses 4 and 5 indicate they do not. I cannot foresee that a role actor would ever state they want to make a complaint about a police officer. If they indicate that they wished to pursue this course of action, the candidate would feel obliged to start taking details. Therefore, the interaction would continue to focus on that aspect, thus preventing the candidate from addressing other issues in the exercise. However, there is no harm in asking the question.

1.4 ... what were comments heard in community. Asking this question would provide you with information relating to the depth of feeling within the general community. The role actor would respond with information that they have overheard comments similar to those contained in the leaflet

Area 2: Community and Customer Focus

This area contains three behavioural statements, the minimum allowed for a competency area. Notice that all are prefixed by 'Outlines'. The scalar for this area is Thorough to Superficial.

2.1 ... will update role actor regarding officers. Tijani is obviously so concerned about the officer's attitude that they have felt the need to contact Chief Inspector Venerdi. Once you have spoken to the officers, Tijani should be updated with the result.

2.2 ... will update role actor regarding leaflets/group. This is similar to behavioural statement 2.1. Tijani is very concerned at the effect the group and leaflets could have on the asylum seekers and the community. They should be kept updated as to the progress of your enquiries.

2.3 ... intention to meet with hostel residents. Trust and confidence needs to be re-established with the asylum seekers. You should do this at the earliest opportunity.

Area 3: Personal Responsibility

This area contains six behavioural statements, the maximum allowed for a competency area. Notice that all are prefixed by 'Outlines'. The scalar for this area is Purposeful to Vague.

I have laid out the competencies **3.1 (... officer's comments unacceptable), 3.2 (... will find out identity of officer) and 3.3 (... will speak to/deal with officer)** in a way that shows how it is possible for you to score more than one behavioural statement in one sentence or consecutively. A candidate could say something along the lines of:

"Do you know who the officers are that attended the robbery report?" **(1.1)**

Role actor response 3.

"I agree the comment was unacceptable **(3.1)**. I will find out who attended the report form our call logs **(3.2)** and deal with them accordingly **(3.3)**. I will then get back to you and let you know how I got on **(2.1)**."

Easy isn't it!

3.4 ... intention to speak to other teams. You may feel this necessary to prevent a reoccurrence of the incident at the hostel.

3.5 ... intention to investigate leaflet/group. You certainly need to ensure that this is carried out. The effect, or potential effect, of the leaflet and the group on the asylum seekers and community has been made clear in the candidate information.

3.6 ... intention to investigate robbery of asylum seeker. There is no indication that this has been done to a satisfactory standard. You could score this behavioural statement by outlining that you will enquire as to the current stage of the enquiry or by reallocating other officers.

Area 4: Strategic Perspective

This area contains four behavioural statements. Notice that all are prefixed by 'Outlines'. The scalar for this area is Purposeful to Vague.

4.1/4.2 ... personal commitment to forum/... organisational commitment to forum. You are new to the division and want to allay any concerns that Tijani may have as regards your or the organisation's commitment to the multi-racial forum.

4.3 ... leaflet is racially motivated/racial incident. Outlining this to Tijani would show how committed you are to ensuring the matter is fully investigated and addressed.

4.4 ... potential implications of leaflet. Examples of implications include attacks on asylum seekers, increase in racial hatred and incidents in the area, disorder in the area and the undermining of the good work the multi-racial forum has achieved.

Area 5: Respect for Race and Diversity

This competency area does not contain behavioural statements. You are assessed across the five-minute interaction against two scalars, in this case Objective to Biased and Sensitive to Insensitive.